*Understanding
Hamlet*

Understanding Hamlet

A study at an advanced level

P. WINDERS, M.A.

HEADMASTER, BROWNEDGE ST. MARY'S SECONDARY SCHOOL, BAMBER BRIDGE
PRESTON.

*Why, look you now, how unworthy
a thing you make of me! you
would play upon me, you would
seem to know my stops, you
would pluck out the heart of my
mystery.*

Hamlet III 2 366

PERGAMON PRESS

A. Wheaton and Company (Educational Publishers), Hennock Road, Exeter EX2 8RP.

Pergamon of Canada Ltd., P.O. Box 9600, Don Mills, Ontario M3C 2T9, Canada.

Pergamon Press (Aust.) Pty Ltd., 19a Boundary Street, Rushcutters Bay, N.S.W. 2011, Australia.

The author and the publisher would be most grateful to receive any comments or suggestions for improving the usefulness of this book.

First edition 1975

Printed in Great Britain by A. Wheaton & Co., Exeter

ISBN 0 08 017777 8 non net
     0 08 018304 2 net

Contents

Acknowledgements

The author wishes to thank the following for their help: The National Computer Centre who provided the flow diagram on page 135; Holte Photographics for the photographs of the Royal Shakespeare Company productions on pages 101–104; the Shakespeare Centre for access to their press cuttings; Peter Hall for the use of his programme notes; Trevor Nunn for his time and for the use of his director's notes; and Marjorie Craven for her gallant efforts in typing the manuscript of this book.

Cover photograph by A. M. Hart.

About this book

This book is written to help the student over those uncertain and sometimes anxious weeks when he makes his first acquaintance with a difficult text at an advanced level. It does not pretend to be all-embracing or exhaustive; merely an introductory book, a skeletal structure on which the student's personal design can be imposed. It will suggest lines along which he ought to be thinking if he is to reach an understanding of the work in question.

The book is divided into two sections. Section 1 aims at opening a range of the topics which will be the student's concern. It attempts to arrange its material in a logical, thematic way which will prove helpful in the organization of essays; the sub-headings provide a simple guide to the progress of the main text and there is cross-reference between relevant parts, although the cross-references are best left at first reading until the student is later searching for specific material. Short critical opinions have been gathered, as appropriate, and applied to the text of the work itself. Finally, two recent productions of Hamlet are considered to show how the ideas generated by literary criticism can be translated into the theatre.

Section 2 has two functions: it focuses attention on details of the text by means of questions on selected passages; and it offers areas for profitable thought or discussion.

At the end of the book there is a short review of publications by those critics whose names are asterisked in Section 1. It is hoped that the student will be stimulated to delve more deeply into the problems which have been dealt with only superficially here.

All line references are to The New Shakespeare edition of *Hamlet*, edited by John Dover Wilson and published by the Cambridge University Press.

Section 1
Approach

Chapter 1

Setting a Course

Embarking on a study of *Hamlet*, we are faced with a task which is difficult and complex but ultimately rewarding. Perhaps we have already begun our studies: we may have read the play and found it puzzling; we may have been recommended to read the opinions of a particular critic about *Hamlet* and have discovered that he spends only one third of his time expounding his own view of the play and the rest in refuting the views of other critics with whom he disagrees and whose work we have not read. Conscientiously we have delved into the library shelves for this further work and found to our dismay that its authors refer to still more legions of critics, all busily disproving each other's theories.

Looking for a way of expressing our deepening bewilderment, we might compare ourselves with a small boat making for port in a rough sea: all the charts indicate hazards ahead but, unfortunately, no two charts agree on either the position or nature of the hazards; we turn to our compass for assurance but find that each reading differs alarmingly from the last.

If we have reached this state of mind it is because we are becoming aware of the problems facing any student of *Hamlet*. The first of these is the sheer volume of published material which the play has inspired. It has been computed that every tenth day of this century has seen the birth of some item of *Hamlet* commentary, and Jan Kott* observed that the mere bibliography of studies devoted to the play is twice the size of Warsaw's telephone directory.

A second problem is an increasing feeling of frustrated irrelevance as we are compelled in the pursuit of our study to focus more and more narrowly on smaller and smaller aspects of the play and, consequently, we become divorced from its overall design. It is in its total dramatic impact that the magic of *Hamlet* lies. Peter Hall[1], who directed a production at Stratford in the mid-sixties, has warned in connection with this play:

> Dismember an evocative Chinese puzzle and you are left with the pieces, not the puzzle.

Eventually, however, when all our armchair dissection is completed, we can reassemble the complete drama by going to see a production of *Hamlet*

---

[1] Peter Hall: Programme notes to Stratford production 1965.

in a theatre, which is the proper place to appreciate any play. It is then that we shall gain our reward.

The Problem that is HAMLET

By far our greatest trouble, however, will lie in keeping a sense of direction. *Hamlet* has been termed a problem play because it does not explicitly turn our thoughts in one particular direction. A problem play, according to Ernest Schanzer[2], is one in which there is:

> a concern with a moral problem which is central to it, presented in such a manner that we are unsure of our moral bearings, so that uncertain and divided responses to it in the minds of the audience are possible or even probable.

As we progress further in this book, we may well conclude that the problem in *Hamlet* is one which spreads beyond this definition, but we shall not be able to deny that the play provokes "uncertain and divided responses."

SOME CONFLICTING VIEWS ON THE PLAY AND ITS CENTRAL CHARACTER

Here are some comments to show the extent and variety of interpretation which *Hamlet* has inspired.

a) C. S. Lewis[3] explains why he thinks it a great work of art:

> The fact that they cannot leave *Hamlet* alone, the continual groping, the sense, unextinguished by over a century of failures, that we have here something of inestimable importance, is surely the best evidence that the real and lasting mystery of our human situation has been greatly depicted.

b) B. Ifor Evans[4] pays tribute to the universal fascination of the play's central character;

> At the centre is Hamlet himself, melancholic, introspective, witty, incomprehensible and gracious, that strange, unaccountable Renaissance prince in whom, by some unfathomable miracle, Everyman, not only in England but wherever the play is enacted, finds the image of his own art.

c) William Hazlitt[5] observed:

> The character of Hamlet is itself a pure effusion of genius.

d) On the other hand Charles Marowitz[6], a young modern director, has been less than polite in his deliberately provocative irritation:

> I despise Hamlet. He is a slob, a talker, an analyzer, a rationalizer. Like the parlour liberal or the paralysed intellectual, he can describe every facet of a problem, yet never pull his finger out. . . . You may think he is a sensitive, well-spoken fellow, but, frankly, he gives me a pain in the ass.

---

[2] Ernest Schanzer: *The Problem Plays of Shakespeare* (Routledge and Kegan Paul) 1963.
[3] C. S. Lewis: *They Asked for a Paper* (Geoffrey Bles.)
[4] B. Ifor Evans: *The Language of Shakespeare's Plays* (Indiana U.P.) 1952.
[5] W. Hazlitt: *Characters of Shakespeare's Plays* 1817 (Reprinted Oxford World Classics) 1916.
[6] C. Marowitz: Preface to *The Marowitz Hamlet* (Penguin) 1970.

e) Obviously a character which can produce such a polarisation of sympathy offers a strong interpretative challenge to any ambitious actor. It is not, therefore, surprising to hear John Dover-Wilson* remark:

> No "part" in the whole repertory of dramatic literature is so certain of success with almost any audience, and is yet open to such a remarkable variety of interpretation. There are as many Hamlets as there are actors who play him; and Bernhardt has proved that even a woman can score a success. Of a role so indeterminate in composition almost any version is possible.

f) Not only is the role of Hamlet capable of innumerable slants but so is the whole play, which makes it a favourite with producers. Peter Hall[7] has this to say:

> *Hamlet* is one of mankind's great images. It turns a new face to each decade. It is a mirror which gives back the reflection of the age that is contemplating it.

g) Although there has been a danger that *Hamlet's* popularity might cause it to be enshrined as inviolable, T. S. Eliot* was brave enough to argue:

> Far from being Shakespeare's masterpiece, the play is most certainly an artistic failure.
> Probably more people have thought *Hamlet* a work of art because they found it interesting, than have found it interesting because it is a work of art.

h) Patrick Crutwell[8] offers us a conclusion to this section:

> The one thing about Hamlet (prince and play) on which all writers are in agreement is the unique extent of their disagreement.

A DIRECTION MARKER

These then are the turbulent waters which we are attempting to navigate. Before we set our course, however, there is a point which we can mark on our charts with reasonable confidence, a piece of background information which will prove very useful later: the sources from which Shakespeare took *Hamlet*.

THE SOURCES OF HAMLET. The basic Hamlet story is a folk-tale originating in Iceland some five hundred years before Shakespeare used it. It was first put into literary form by the Danish historian, Saxo Grammaticus, probably in the 13th century although his account was not printed until the 15th century.

In the 16th century Saxo's version was translated into French by Belleforest, but this is unlikely to have been one of Shakespeare's direct sources because it was not itself translated into English until 1608, whereas *Hamlet* is dated 1600–1601.

---

[7] Peter Hall: *op cit.*
[8] P. Cruttwell: 'The Morality of Hamlet – "Sweet Prince" or "Arrant Knave"?' from *Hamlet* ed. J. Russell Brown and Bernard Harris, Stratford-upon-Avon Studies 5 (Edward Arnold) 1963.

There was a Hamlet play of the 1580's based on Belleforest and usually attributed to Thomas Kyd. No manuscript of this play has survived but we know a little about it from contemporary references and it is likely to have been available to Shakespeare as a source. The scholars refer to this missing play as the *Ur-Hamlet*.

The basic elements of Shakespeare's plot are present in Saxo's account: a king is murdered by his brother, and the brother takes the throne and marries the dead man's widow, called Gerutha. Her son, Amleth, decides to take revenge on his uncle and simulates madness in order to protect himself (at one point he enters pretending to be a cock, flapping his arms like wings). The king becomes suspicious of this behaviour and devises sanity tests for Amleth, who evades them. A beautiful girl is sent to spy on him. He is further spied upon while talking to his mother and, having discovered the spy, he kills him, dismembers the body and feeds it to the pigs. He is sent to England, intentionally to his death, but changes a letter so that his two companions are killed in his place. After a year's absence, he returns in disguise, sets fire to the palace, kills his uncle with a sword and succeeds to the throne.

The ingredients of *Hamlet* are recognizable, but Shakespeare has transformed the crudity of the original into a more mature dramatic design.

THE PRINCE OR THE PLAY?

We must now decide in which direction to set our initial course.

We could begin by accepting A. C. Bradley's* statement that "the whole story (of *Hamlet*) turns upon the peculiar character of the hero", and concentrate on elucidating that character. In doing so we should be following the approach of 19th century and early 20th century criticism, which often looked on plays as if they were psychological novels, with the characters to be regarded as having existences so real that not only could they be analysed within the textual confines of the play but they could be projected as living beyond the scope of the drama. This type of approach tended more and more to isolate the play from the theatre; it reached its extreme form in William Hazlitt's[9] comment:

> We do not like to see our author's plays acted, and least of all, *Hamlet*. There is no play that suffers so much in being transferred to the stage.

This critical approach might be summed up in the question, "What is the true state of Hamlet's mind?" with the further implicit assumption that if we can answer that question, we shall understand what the play is about.

Modern criticism has tried to redress any imbalance by emphasizing the theatrical approach to *Hamlet* and by regarding the play as a total dramatic design from which it is wrong to extract the prince for special microscopic examination. Harry Levin* agrees that *Hamlet* without Hamlet would be

[9] W. Hazlitt: *op cit.*

unthinkable but goes on to claim that "Hamlet without *Hamlet* has been thought about all too much". L. C. Knights* applauded the:

> salutary tendency of recent criticism to see Shakespeare's tragedies as imaginative wholes rather than as dramatic constructions designed to exhibit "character", however fascinating.

and J. Dover Wilson* had no doubt that the

> psychological critics . . . have one and all begun at the wrong end by attempting to solve the riddle of Hamlet's character before making sure that they understand the play in which he is the principal figure.

This critical approach might be summed up in the question "What is the play about?" with the further implicit assumption that if we can answer that question, then we shall be in a position to understand Hamlet himself.

We shall choose to embark on our *Hamlet* voyage by trying to familiarise ourselves with the play's overall dramatic concept before going on to consider the nature of its central character. By doing this we shall be in a position to find our way about the play generally before being driven to a closer examination of the text. Even as we adopt this approach, we realise and apologise for the artificiality which is inherent in any division between character and drama; we can only excuse it on the grounds that it will help us to ease ourselves gradually into the complexities of the play. We promise to bear always in mind that "the man (Hamlet) and the experience (*Hamlet*) go together".

Chapter 2

What is the Play about?

It is time, then, to consider the ideas which the play is designed to express. So we ask the deceptively simple questions: what is the play about? what was in Shakespeare's mind when he wrote *Hamlet?*

Here are four useful approaches:

    a) It is a revenge play.
    b) It is a play concerned with the nature of evil.
    c) It is a play about death.
    d) It is a play about "not knowing for sure".

In the event, of course, *Hamlet* is about all of these things and again we feel conscious of the essentially artificial division which we find it necessary to adopt at this stage.

A Revenge Play

Hamlet lies directly in the tradition of the revenge tragedy, which was a common-place in the Elizabethan and Jacobean theatre. In the usual run of that tradition the hero would be appraised of the situation (ghosts were a popular device), he would accept his duty, and the interest of the plot would be in the way in which he overcame any material obstacles (such as bodyguards) in the path of his revenge, and in the final manner (bloody? cunning? horrifying? involved?) in which the revenge was accomplished. In essence the revenge tragedy was formed in the mould of Seneca, a Roman playwright whose plays were characterized by horrific incidents, ghosts, bloody actions and ranting speeches. As such, its purpose was to thrill and to intrigue.

A popular revenge play of Shakespeare's time was *The Spanish Tragedy* by Thomas Kyd, in which Hieronimo is called upon to avenge the murder of his son, done to death by Lorenzo, brother of Bel-imperia, the son's lover. Father delays, often lamenting his lot in passionate outbursts akin to madness. He and Bel-imperia finally exact their revenge in a play-within-the-play by doing in earnest what the victim expects to be make-believe.

Some ingredients of *Hamlet* are recognisable here.

SHAKESPEARE'S EARLIER REVENGE PLAY: *TITUS ANDRONICUS*

Earlier in his career Shakespeare had tried his hand at a revenge play in *Titus Andronicus*. A résumé of the plot suggests that it adheres very closely to the spirit of the Senecan drama.

The successful Roman general, Titus Andronicus, returns from victory over the Goths, but bringing yet another personal loss, the death of the twenty-first of his twenty-five sons. With Titus' approval, his four remaining sons exact a sacrifical revenge for the slaughter of their brother by cutting to pieces and burning one of the sons of Tamora, the captive queen of the Goths. Tamora's other two sons, Chiron and Demetrius, quietly swear to to watch for the "opportunity of sharp revenge".

Titus' daughter, Lavinia, on the point of being betrothed to the newly elected Emperor of Rome, is seized, willingly, by her lover, Bassianus, the Emperor's brother, and they make off together. Titus attempts to pursue them and, finding his way barred by his son, Mutius, stabs him to death. Only three sons left! The Emperor, Saturninus, now marries Tamora and she, in her new position of power, swears counter-revenge on Titus and the remnants of his family:

I'll find a day to massacre them all.

The arch-villain who will master-mind this vengeance is Aaron, Tamora's Moorish lover, the epitome of Machiavellian cunning and vice. He channels the energies of Chiron and Demetrius, both full of lustful rivalry for Lavinia, by suggesting that, as a reward for murdering Bassianus, they might dispose of Lavinia as they wish. Accordingly, they stab Bassianus and drag Lavinia away to be raped. Bassianus' body is dumped in a pit into which Aaron then persuades two of Titus' sons, Quintus and Martius, conveniently to fall (sic) so that he can arrange for suspicion of the murder to fall with equal convenience upon them. The Emperor being duly deceived, Quintus and Martius are arrested and condemned to death. Meanwhile, Chiron and Demetrius, having ravished Lavinia, take steps to ensure the secrecy of their deeds by chopping off her hands and cutting out her tongue.

There follow passages of appropriately hyperbolic anguish in which Titus laments the plight of his daughter and pleads for the life of his sons until eventually a decision arrives from the Emperor: Titus must cut off his hand in exchange for Quintus and Martius. With true Roman strength of mind Titus allows Aaron to axe his hand and convey it to the Emperor, in return for which (O treachery how predictable!) he receives the severed heads of his sons.

The revenge being exacted by Tamora is sickening in its cruelty and, not surprisingly, in its turn goads Titus and his one living son, Lucius, to plan counter-counter-revenge. By writing in the dust with a stick, Lavinia is able to reveal the identity of her attackers, thus giving Titus a more clearly defined target; whilst Lucius sets off to raise an army of Goths to attack Rome.

Following the latest deaths in his family Titus apparently goes mad, showing this by shooting arrows into the air with messages to the gods affixed. Whether his madness is genuine or merely a device to obscure his plottings may be problematical, but Tamora is sufficiently convinced of the authenticity of Titus' distraction to visit him disguised as the morality figure Revenge with her sons appropriately as Rapine and Murder, in order to persuade Titus to divert Lucius from the battlefield to the conference-table. Titus, pretending to be deceived by the disguises, agrees to bring Lucius to a sort of working lunch if Chiron and Demetrius will stay with Titus, which they do; whereupon they are seized and in the presence of the mutilated Lavinia have their throats cut. Such a quick and simple dispatch, however, does not constitute a full and savoury revenge; Titus has a more subtle device. Chiron and Demetrius are to be finely chopped, delicately sauced and served to their mother at the ensuing lunch as a sort of Gothic pie. The feast provides a fittingly violent climax to the play: Tamora becomes an unsuspecting infantivore; Titus formally executes Lavinia to end her life of shame; and in a sequence of exchanges following the revelation of the grisly nature of Tamora's repast, Titus stabs Tamora, Saturninus stabs Titus and Lucius kills Saturninus.

This outline of the plot, atmospherically supported by frequent and blood-curdling references to vengeance and by long speeches full of exaggerated emotions, reflects the substance of *Titus Andronicus*, a play in which the sole purpose of the author is to stimulate and explore feelings of horror and terror in his audience.

REVENGE ELEMENTS IN *HAMLET*

Hamlet's kinship with revenge melodrama can be similarly demonstrated by summarising its plot.

The play opens with an atmosphere of suspense:

> For this relief much thanks, 'tis bitter cold   I i 8
> And I am sick at heart.

There is a feeling that something is wrong: the ghost appears, to harrow us with fear and wonder, and, according to Horatio:

> This bodes some strange eruption to our state.   I i 69

Next we see Hamlet himself, gloomy amidst the splendour of the Danish court, disillusioned to the point of considering suicide. But whatever has caused him already to feel bitter, there is worse to come. The ghost speaks to Hamlet, bringing a blast of hell into the play, and reveals the murder. Here are blood and intrigue as young Hamlet takes on the duty of revenge. He assumes madness to assist him in his task and, yet more intriguing, it soon becomes impossible to distinguish between what is pretence and what is reality.

Claudius, suspicious of Hamlet, employs spies to "sift" the prince's behaviour, and Hamlet parries their attempts with his own brand of cunning.

Whilst Claudius is busy probing Hamlet, Hamlet is preparing to expose Claudius by means of the play-within-the-play, a tense and exciting scene which ends by convincing the prince of his uncle's guilt. But even now, the expected climax of the play is delayed: Hamlet accidentally kills Polonius and is consequently despatched to his death in England, only to escape by a combination of his intelligence and an extraordinary stroke of good fortune.

Meanwhile, Ophelia goes mad, offering a marked contrast to Hamlet's earlier distraction, and commits suicide by drowning. Laertes bursts into the palace to offer the point of his sword to Claudius's throat, but is easily manipulated to divert his anger towards Hamlet. Hamlet returns from England, discourses, "too curiously" in Horatio's opinion, on the inhabitants of a graveyard, and fights with Laertes in Ophelia's grave.

The play concludes with Claudius's three-pronged Machiavellian plot to dispose of Hamlet – the sword unbated, its point envenomed, and a poisoned cup. Evil, however, has the habit of stinging those who try to use it. Gertrude and Laertes, as well as Hamlet, are killed by Claudius's plot and, finally, Hamlet achieves his revenge by running Claudius through with the lethal sword and forcing the poisoned wine down his throat. A catalogue

> Of carnal, bloody and unnatural acts,   V 2 379
> Of accidental judgements, casual slaughters,
> Of deaths put on by cunning and forced cause,
> And, in this upshot, purposes mistook
> Fall'n on th'inventors' heads. . . . .

to delight the most avid Elizabethan lover of melodrama.

As in *Titus Andronicus* the revenge aspect in *Hamlet* is emphasized by frequent repetition but in the Roman play the numerous incidents of vengeance follow consequentially one from another; in *Hamlet* the various threats of revenge are made by different characters in different circumstances and are reflective of each other rather than connected. (Shakespeare uses the same mirror method in *King Lear* where in writing about the breakdown of family ties, he shows the widespread application of his theme by tracing its parallel effect in two families simultaneously).

The main revenge action in *Hamlet* is the ghost's commission to "revenge his foul and most unnatural murder", a commission which the prince accepts enthusiastically:

> Haste me to know't, that I with wings as swift   I 5 29
> As meditation or the thoughts of love,
> May sweep to my revenge.

Interestingly, the vow of acceptance is made in the passion of the moment with no time for thought and the actual carrying out of the vow is achieved only in similar mood. The rest of the play can be seen as a struggle by Hamlet against the convention of revenge which we have seen so crudely worked out in *Titus Andronicus*, with which the Elizabethan audience would be familiar and to which they might reasonably have expected Hamlet to conform. They must have been puzzled, for, if Titus and Tamora pursue their revenge with wholehearted satisfaction and relish, Hamlet certainly does not. He finds it easier that he should:

>like a whore unpack my heart with words   II 2 589

than act and, despite his claim to be

>proud, revengeful, ambitious,   III 1 125

and despite the various self-generated spurs to his dull revenge, he stands as a marked contrast to Titus (see Chapter 4, which considers Hamlet's delay in perpetrating his avowed revenge).

The call for vengeance from father to son is reflected in other relationships in the play. The news of Polonius' death can hardly have sunk into Laertes' brain before that dutiful son has his sword at Claudius' throat and is prepared to sacrifice his own happiness both in this world and the one to come:

>only I'll be revenged   IV 5 135
>Most throughly for my father.

(Page 63) Similarly, young Fortinbras is prepared to raise a rebel army to avenge the death and defeat of his father. Again, even in the seemingly incidental speech of the first player the revenge theme figures as Pyrrhus, son of the dead Achilles, stimulated by "a roused vengeance", minces the limbs of Priam. (It is worth noting that the language of this speech resembles that of *Titus Antronicus* more than it resembles anything else in *Hamlet*).

As in *Titus Andronicus* the revenge plots are supported by some atmospheric passages. One thinks of

>In the most high and palmy state of Rome,   I 1 113
>A little ere the mightiest Julius fell,
>The graves stood tenantless, and the sheeted dead
>Did squeak and gibber in the Roman streets,
>And even the like precurse of fierce events,
>As harbingers preceding still the fates
>And prologue to the omen coming on,
>Have heaven and earth together demonstrated
>Unto our climatures and countrymen,
>As stars with trains of fire and dews of blood,

Disasters in the sun; and the moist star,
Upon whose influence Neptune's empire stands,
Was sick almost to doomsday with eclipse.

and:

> 'Tis now the very witching time of night,
> When churchyards yawn, and hell itself breathes out
> Contagion to this world: now could I drink hot blood,
> And do such bitter business as the day
> Would quake to look on . . . .

III 2 391

We can, then, point to a similarity between *Titus Andronicus* and *Hamlet*: they have some common ground. But to say this, without considerable qualification, is as misleading as to say that a terraced house in Wigan and Buckingham Palace are similar because they are both dwellings. Our short résumé of *Titus Andronicus* told us a lot about that play; our equivalent review of *Hamlet*, on the other hand, has told us very little. (It is significant that it was possible to summarise *Hamlet* in half the space of *Titus Andronicus*). The flesh which Shakespeare has moulded on to the bare bones of a revenge play is what gives *Hamlet* its value. (Page 25).

The Presence of Evil in the World

We are given to understand that, before the murder of Old Hamlet, Denmark was a place of sunshine, vitality, stability and fair prospects for everyone. Hamlet admired his father and seemed busy educating himself to become a worthy popular successor. Ophelia describes the excellent qualities of her lover in earlier and happier days in terms applicable to a courteous and sociable Renaissance prince:

> O, what a noble mind is here o'erthrown!
> The courtier's, soldier's, scholar's, eye, tongue, sword,
> Th'expectancy and rose of the fair state,
> The glass of fashion, and the mould of form,
> Th'observed of all observers . . . .

III 1 153

Indeed Fortinbras testifies at the close of the play to Hamlet's brilliant promise:

> For he was likely, had he been put on,
> To have proved most royal . . . .

V 2 395

At Ophelia's graveside, Gertrude laments that things did not turn out as they might have done in a more fortunate world:

I hoped thou shouldst have been my Hamlet's wife: V 1 238
I thought thy bride-bed to have decked, sweet maid,
And not have strewed thy grave.

All in all, the period before the play opens appears to have been sound and potentially prosperous.

DENMARK AN UNHEALTHY STATE...

The murder of Hamlet's father, however, releases into the body politic a symbolic poison as powerful as the one which Shakespeare so vividly describes acting in Old Hamlet's bloodstream:

The leperous distilment, whose effect   I 5 64
Holds such an enmity with blood of man,
That swift as quicksilver it courses through
The natural gates and alleys of the body,
And with a sudden vigour it doth posset
And curd, like eager droppings into milk,
The thin and wholesome blood; so did it mine,
And a most instant tetter barked about
Most lazar-like with vile and loathsome crust
All my smooth body...

The appearance of the ghost is the first manifestation of the poison and Horatio and Marcellus realise this:

Horatio: This bodes some strange eruption to our state.   I 1 69

and:

Marcellus: Something is rotten in the state of Denmark.   I 4 90

Something indeed! What was once a healthy constitution is henceforth a "prison", a place of spying and watching; a sickly and decadent environment in which the people are sycophantic, untrustworthy, untrusting and cynical.

✓. FULL OF SPIES AND SYCOPHANTS

Polonius, Rosencrantz and Guildenstern, and Osric are representative of this new sordid Denmark (Claudius is a more complex character to be dealt with later).

POLONIUS. Polonius is often played as a figure of fun with his excessive punning on the word "tender" in I 3 and his frequent long-windedness.

He becomes so involved in his own speech to Reynaldo that he forgets what he is saying:

> what was I about to say? II 1 48
> By the mass I was about to say something.
> Where did I leave?

and even his apology when Gertrude has rebuked his verbosity lacks brevity:

> Madam, I swear I use no art at all. II 2 96
> That he is mad 'tis true, 'tis true, 'tis pity,
> And pity 'tis 'tis true – a foolish figure,
> But farewell it, for I will use no art.

Hamlet has no difficulty in making fun of his obsequiousness in the conversation about cloud shapes in III 2 and easily makes a fool of him in II 2 (Page 46).

There is, however, a nastier and more serious side to the portrayal of Polonius. He is a dangerous meddler: he cynically sends Reynaldo to spy on Laertes (II 1); he jumps to hurried conclusions about Ophelia's relationship with Hamlet, suggesting that the prince is merely toying with her, and orders her to repel his advances (I 3); even when proved wrong, he rushes to meddle again by displaying Hamlet's love-letters as evidence of the cause of Hamlet's madness (II 1). Worst of all, he is prepared to use Ophelia as bait:

> At such a time I'll loose my daughter to him. II 2 162
> Be you and I behind an arras then,
> Mark the encounter, if he love her not,
> And be not from his reason fall'n there on,
> Let me be no assistant for a state,
> But keep a farm, and carters . . . .

thereby exposing her to a savage attack from Hamlet, which could well be the first step towards her suicide; and, callousness personified, he remains unmoved by Ophelia's distress whilst he plans yet more spying with Claudius. This, however, turns out to be Polonius's last bit of meddling; he finally gains his reward on the end of Hamlet's sword and at the same time two potted character sketches by way of obituary:

> Thou wretched, rash, intruding fool, farewell! III 4 31

and:

Is now most still, most secret, and most grave,
Who was in life a foolish prating knave . . .

Not every producer sees Polonius as a fool. Peter Hall[1] writes:

> He is not a doddering old fool but the kind of tough, shrewd establishment
> figure you can still meet in St. James's; a man who sends himself up, and uses
> his silly humour as a weapon.

And John Dover Wilson* recalls a modern-dress production by the
Birmingham Repertory Company, in which one of the best features was:

> the playing of Polonius as a dapper and exceedingly shrewd diplomatist, a
> worthy "assistant for the state", but ageing and allowing his shrewdness to
> o'er-reach itself.

Perhaps Polonius's most important function is, like that of most of the
characters in this play, to act as a contrast to Hamlet. Polonius is content
with façades: his platitudinous advice to Laertes in I 3 indicates a superficial morality. Hamlet, on the other hand, penetrates beyond appearance
to the reality beneath: he hates the shallowness of which Polonius is a prime
example:

Seems, madam! nay it is, I know not 'seems'.   I 2 76
'Tis not alone my inky cloak, good mother,
Nor customary suits of solemn black,
Nor windy suspiration of forced breath,
No, nor the fruitful river in the eye,
Nor the dejected haviour of the visage,
Together with all forms, modes, shapes of grief,
That can denote me truly. These indeed seem,
For they are actions that a man might play,
But I have that within which passes show,
These but the trappings and the suits of woe.

Polonius accepts his surroundings without understanding them; Hamlet
understands but cannot accept.

ROSENCRANTZ AND GUILDENSTERN. In terms of dramatic function, Rosencrantz and Guildenstern are similar to Polonius. Firstly, they are syco-
phants: they reply to Claudius's request to them to "sift" Hamlet in the
most servile tones:

Both your majesties   II 2 26
Might by the sovereign power you have of us,

---

[1] Peter Hall: *op cit.*

> Put your dread pleasures more into command
> Than to entreaty.

The inversion of their two names at this point by Claudius and Gertrude suggests that they are totally indistinguishable one from the other. Later, they accept another commission with oily flattery of Claudius:

> Most holy and religious fear it is   III 3 8
> To keep those many many bodies safe
> That live and feed upon your majesty.

Again, like Polonius, they become part of Claudius's intelligence service, but not a very effective part because they are immediately transparent to Hamlet:

> Were you not sent for?   II 2 277

They admit this to be the case, and Hamlet goes on to show his contempt for them by fooling Guildenstern with the recorder; foolery which culminates in the bitter rebuke:

> 'Sblood, do you think I am easier to be played   III 2 372
> on than a pipe?

and his disgust is even more obvious in his later description of their sordid employment:

> Hamlet: Besides, to be demanded of a sponge,   IV 2 12
>   what replication should be made by the
>   son of a king?
> Rosencrantz: Take you me for a sponge, my lord?
> Hamlet: Ay, sir, that soaks up the king's counten-
>   ance, his rewards, his authorities. But
>   such officers do the king best service in
>   the end, he keeps them like an apple in
>   the corner of his jaw, first mouthed to
>   be last swallowed – when he needs what
>   you have gleaned, it is but squeezing
>   you, and, sponge, you shall be dry
>   again.

Eventually, as with Polonius, their eagerness to help Claudius leads to their death. Perhaps they might have learned from the earlier recorder incident that Hamlet was too clever for them, and that

'Tis dangerous when the baser nature comes   V 2 60
Between the pass and fell incensèd points
Of mighty opposites.

The important factor about their death is that it shows Hamlet at his most callous: he hates their lack of integrity and their willingness to be used:

Why, man, they did make love to this employment,   V 2 57
They are not near my conscience, their defeat
Does by their own insinuation grow.

It ought to be pointed out that in one way Rosencrantz and Guildenstern differ from Polonius: there is every indication that Polonius has always been a time-server whilst presumably, as chosen friends and intimate companions of Hamlet in former, happier days, Rosencrantz and Guildenstern were wholesome creatures. Perhaps we ought to regard them as victims of the corrupting nature of evil (Page 17).

The interpretation of Rosencrantz and Guildenstern can vary considerably according to different productions: sometimes they are seen as foppish and intellectual, sometimes as dangerous informers and spies. One director[2] wrote:

> They are not a couple of villains, but two men caught in the mechanism of politics, who are not as clever as they think and become easy tools of the expert politician, Claudius.

OSRIC. Towards the end of the play the "waterfly", Osric, succeeds to the role of the departed Rosencrantz and Guildenstern. He is a superb pen-portrait of a sycophantic courtier, foppish and effeminate. In V 2 Hamlet enjoys exposing Osric's nervous obsequiousness in the dialogue about his hat and the weather: an incident reminiscent of Polonius and the clouds. Hamlet sums up his servility in one of the sharpest comments in the play:

A' did comply, sir, with his dug before a' sucked it.   V 2 188

IMAGES OF HYPOCRISY. The presentation of these characters as symptoms of the general sickness of Denmark is supported by the thematic imagery of the play, which deals partly with hypocrisy. Gertrude is described by the ghost as "my seeming-virtuous queen"; Polonius talks in terms of hiding one's evil nature beneath a facade of religion:

'Tis too much proved, that with devotion's visage   III 1 47
And pious action we do sugar o'er
The devil himself.

[2] *ibid.*

Claudius questions the genuineness of Laertes' love for his father: is it sincere or mere show?

> Or are you like the painting of a sorrow,   IV 7 107
> A face without a heart?

Cosmetics are seen as part of female deception, a means of hiding blemishes by a beautiful surface. Hamlet viciously attacks Ophelia:

> I have heard of your paintings too, well enough. God   III 1 145
> hath given you one face and you make yourselves
> another,

and later, musing over Yorick's skull, he inveighs cynically against such false faces with the words

> Get you to my lady's chamber, and tell her, let her   V 1 188
> paint an inch thick, to this favour she must come.

Claudius refers to the covering up of his own crimes in similar terms:

> The harlot's cheek, beautied with plast'ring art,   III 1 51
> Is not more ugly to the thing that helps it,
> Than is my deed to my most painted word . . .

EVIL AS A DISEASE

So, there is evil in Denmark. But what does the play tell us about the nature of evil? Firstly, evil is contagious and blights the good in life. H. D. F. Kitto[3] wrote:

> Evil, once started on its course, will so work as to attack and overthrow imparti-
> ally the good and the bad.

Evil is like a disease which attacks and destroys the healthy parts of the body and can spread to epidemic proportions if unchecked. Hamlet uses the phrase

>   hell itself breathes out   III 2 392
> Contagion to this world:

and elsewhere talks of the "dram of evil" which can consume the whole "noble substance".

---

[3] H. D. F. Kitto: *Form and Meaning in Drama* (Methuen) 1959.

IMAGES OF DISEASE. In fact the play is full of disease imagery. Hamlet cannot give a "wholesome" answer because his "wit's diseas'd". He accuses his mother of not facing the reality of the evil course she has chosen in marrying Claudius:

> for love of grace,   III 4 144
> Lay not that flattering unction to your soul,
> That not your trespass but my madness speaks,
> It will but skin and film the ulcerous place,
> Whilst rank corruption mining all within
> Infects unseen.

Claudius says that, in ignoring Hamlet's madness, he has,

> like the owner of a foul disease,   IV 1 21
> To keep it from divulging, let it feed
> Even on the pith of life . . .

In that these two images refer to the hiding of disease, they can be connected with the imagery of hypocrisy noted above. Ironically, it is Claudius, the originator of the sickness, who speaks mostly in terms of disease. He says of Hamlet:

> For like the hectic in my blood he rages   IV 3 65

and justifies his sending of Hamlet to England by the words:

> Diseases desperate grown   IV 3 9
> By desperate appliance are relieved,
> Or not at all.

The disease of Denmark is "desperate grown" and the only remedy is a major operation. Unfortunately, as we cut away the cancered cells, we cannot avoid destroying healthy ones. Thus, in cutting out the evil elements in Denmark, the more or less innocent (Ophelia, Hamlet, Laertes and, possibly, Gertrude, Polonius and Rosencrantz and Guildenstern) must also suffer the knife.

AN OPERATION TO CUT OUT EVIL, WITH HAMLET AN UNWILLING SURGEON. The operation might have been a less devastating success had the surgeon been more expert and less unwilling to perform it. But, certainly, Hamlet is the wrong man for the job and knows it; only minutes after being given the task of revenge by the ghost, he says:

> The time is out of joint, O cursèd spite,   I 5 188
> That ever I was born to set it right!

He is a reluctant avenger; unlike other tragic heroes, who help to move themselves into their tragic situations, Hamlet's is imposed upon him (Page 26). Another view is that Hamlet becomes overwhelmed and paralysed by the weight of evil. Certainly we shall see how Hamlet becomes tainted by the contagious mood of his surroundings (Page 49).

Wilson Knight* takes an unsympathetic view of Hamlet's unfittedness for his task. Pursuing the idea of Hamlet himself being blighted by evil, he suggests that an attempt by a sick soul to create harmony is doomed to failure. He goes further and sees Hamlet as a cynical and corrupting influence on a world which is "except for the original murder of Hamlet's father, one of healthy and robust life, good nature, humour, romantic strength, and welfare". Murder is, however, a rather large exception (cf. Claudius. Page 59).

Whatever Hamlet's condition, however, whatever his intentions, his actions (or lack of them) certainly contribute in varying degrees to eight deaths in the play; not the mark of a good surgeon.

Death

C. S. Lewis remarked that "in a sense, the subject of *Hamlet* is death"; which is something of a truism since so many Elizabethan and Jacobean plays are concerned with death, those ages being preoccupied with death as our age seems to be preoccupied with sexual behaviour; each age exploring its particular fetish on every conceivable occasion. Working through Shakespeare's plays one can recognise the common properties of death which are manifested so strongly in *Hamlet*.

1) death as a welcome release from a harsh world,
2) the corruption of the body in the grave
and, most dominant,
3) the waste of life.

DEATH AS A RELEASE

Hamlet's first words alone on stage are full of world-weariness and indicative of the death wish:

> O, that this too too sullied flesh would melt, I 2 129
> Thaw and resolve itself into a dew,
> Or that the Everlasting had not fixed
> His canon 'gainst self-slaughter. O God, God,
> How weary, stale, flat, and unprofitable
> Seem to me all the uses of this world!

and parts of the long soliloquy beginning "To be or not to be" express the certainty that this life is full of misery and vexation of spirit:

> For who would bear the whips and scorns of time, III 1 70
> Th'oppressor's wrong, the proud man's contumely,

The pangs of disprized love, the law's delay,
The insolence of office, and the spurns
That patient merit of th'unworthy takes,
When he himself might his quietus make
With a bare bodkin; who would fardels bear,
To grunt and sweat under a weary life . . .

If the alternative to these earthly tribulations is to be a blissful reward in heaven, then is death indeed a benefit, as the dirge from *Cymbeline* suggests:

Fear no more the heat o' the sun
Nor the furious winter's rages
Thou thy worldly task hast done
Home art gone and ta'en thy wages.

Even if the expectation of bliss hereafter were to be disappointed and we achieved only the oblivion of a dreamless sleep, still the escape would be worthwhile:

To die, to sleep—   III 1 60
No more, and by a sleep to say we end
The heart-ache, and the thousand natural shocks
That flesh is heir to; 'tis a consummation
Devoutly to be wished to die to sleep!

a point of view expressed so well by the Duke in *Measure for Measure*, III 1:

Reason thus with life:
If I do lose thee, I do lose a thing
That none but fools would keep: a breath thou art,
Servile to all the skyey influences,
That dost this habitation where thou keep'st
Hourly afflict: merely, thou art death's fool,
For him thou labour'st by thy flight to shun,
And yet runn'st toward him still . . . . Thou art not noble,
For all th'accommodations that thou bear'st,
Are nursed by baseness . . . . Thou'rt by no means valiant,
For thou dost fear the soft and tender fork
Of a poor worm: thy best of rest is sleep,
And that thou oft provok'st, yet grossly fear'st
Thy death, which is no more . . . . Thou art not thyself,
For thou exist'st on many a thousand grains
That issue out of dust . . . . Happy thou art not,
For what thou hast not, still thou striv'st to get,
And what thou hast, forget'st . . . . Thou art not certain,

For thy complexion shifts to strange effects,
After the moon . . . . If thou art rich, thou'rt poor,
For like an ass whose back with ingots bows,
Thou bear'st thy heavy riches but a journey,
And death unloads thee . . . . Friend hast thou none,
For thine own bowels, which do call thee sire,
The mere effusion of thy proper loins,
Do curse the gout, serpigo, and the rheum,
For ending thee no sooner . . . . Thou hast nor youth nor age,
But as it were an after-dinner's sleep,
Dreaming on both – for all thy blessèd youth
Becomes as agéd, and doth beg the alms
Of palsied eld: and when thou art old and rich,
Thou hast neither heat, affection, limb, nor beauty,
To make thy riches pleasant . . . . What's yet in this,
That bears the name of life? Yet in this life
Lie hid moe thousand deaths; yet death we fear,
That makes these odds all even.

Unfortunately for Hamlet, the simple expedient of quitting life when it becomes intolerable is rendered less happy a solution by a lack of conclusive evidence about man's posthumous destination:

To sleep, perchance to dream, ay there's the rub,   III 1 65
For in that sleep of death what dreams may come
When we have shuffled off this mortal coil
Must give us pause – there's the respect
That makes calamity of so long life . . . .
. . . the dread of something after death,
The undiscovered country, from whose bourn
No traveller returns, puzzles the will,
And makes us rather bear those ills we have,
Than fly to others that we know not of.

(see also Page 32). Furthermore, there are indications that it is offensive to seek death before one's natural time (Ophelia is allowed only "maimed rites" at her burial) and that offence might be punished. Claudio in *Measure for Measure* III 1 vividly expresses the fears which man has to reckon with in facing death:

Ay, but to die, and go we know not where,
To lie in cold obstruction, and to rot,
This sensible warm motion – to become
A kneaded clod; and the delighted spirit
To bathe in fiery floods, or to reside

In thrilling region of thick-ribbéd ice,
To be imprisoned in the viewless winds
And blown with restless violence round about
The pendent world . . . or to be worse than worst
Of those that lawless and incertain thoughts
Imagine howling – 'tis too horrible . . . .
The weariest and most loathéd worldly life
That age, ache, penury, and imprisonment
Can lay on nature – is a paradise
To what we fear of death.

CORRUPTION IN THE GRAVE

Hamlet cannot be sure of an after-life for man; (he seems to ignore the evidence of the ghost in I 5), but he has evidence of what happens to the body after death. He takes a morbid pleasure in thinking and talking about decay. He pictures the worms feeding on the putrescent Polonius and relates the gruesome tale to show "how a king may go a progress through the guts of a beggar". The graveyard scene is full of grotesque references to the rotting of the dead body. "How long will a man lie i' th' earth ere he rot?" asks Hamlet. The reply is symptomatic of the times:

> Faith, if a' be not rotten before a' die, as we have   V 1 159
> many pocky corses now-a-days that will scarce hold
> the laying in . . . .

He toys with Yorick's skull and muses that this smelly object is all that remains of "a fellow of infinite jest".

> Where be your gibes now? Your gambols, your songs,
> your flashes of merriment, that were wont to set the
> table on a roar?

THE WASTE OF LIFE

Probably the most significant questions asked about death in Shakespeare's plays are those which regard death as a waste of the potential in life; witness Fortinbras' final words over Hamlet's body:

> Bear Hamlet like a soldier to the stage,   V 2 394
> For he was likely, had he been put on,
> To have proved most royal;

The pessimistic side of tragedy lies in the fact that the conquest of evil requires the sacrifice of good. (Page 18). Granted, then, that Hamlet is mindful of the corrosive effect of the grave and the uncertainty of the soul's destination, it is none the less the negation of life which troubles him most.

He recognises that to follow the code of revenge is to unleash the "lean abhorred monster", death, to feed indiscriminately on good and evil, including, by convention, himself. This is perhaps the substance of Hamlet's struggle against being embroiled in the act of vengeance, and the explanation of his frequent self-accusations of cowardice, as he torments his mind to discover whether the positiveness of action will outweigh the negation of inevitable death. There is a powerful irony – and one which conveys the impotence of man to dictate the consequences of his own reasoned acts – in the fact that Hamlet's conscientious torment results in at least as much waste of life as would have arisen from a prompt acquiescence to the revenge morality. With no hindrance from Hamlet, and not a little help, death cuts an increasingly violent course through the play, culminating in the words of Fortinbras:

> O proud death,   V 2 362
> What feast is toward in thine eternal cell,
> That thou so many princes at a shot
> So bloodily hast struck?

The consideration of death in *Hamlet* reaches a crescendo in the graveyard scene, in which Hamlet gives free range to his morbid speculation. There is significance in the placing of this scene, immediately before a very changed Hamlet re-enters court life prepared for the final resolution of the play (Page 29).

'Not Knowing for Sure'

Hamlet cannot reach any certain conclusion about an after-life, and this doubt is just one example of the many questions and searching for answers in *Hamlet*. "It is", says Bernard Lott (editor of *Hamlet* in the New Swan Shakespeare), "a play about not knowing for sure". C. S. Lewis notices "a curious groping and tapping of thoughts"; it is a play "full of anxiety. The world of *Hamlet* is a world where one has lost one's way". There are many questions posed. What should a man believe? How should he behave? "What should such fellows as I do crawling between heaven and earth?" Is man to act according to his god-like faculties or is he to follow the lower code which most of humanity seems willing to accept? Perhaps this is Hamlet's predicament; he is a reluctant avenger because he is in a dilemma about whether his task is a moral duty or a temptation to wrong-doing. "How can man secure justice except by committing injustice, and how can he act without outraging the very conscience which demands that he should act?" asks Helen Gardner[4]. It is an excellent quandary, beautifully expressed by Pope in his *Essay on Man*:

[4] Helen Gardner: *The Business of Criticism* (O.U.P.) 1959.

In doubt to act or rest;
In doubt to deem himself a god, or beast;
In doubt his mind or body to prefer;
Born but to die, and reas'ning but to err.

Hamlet goes on questioning but becomes increasingly baffled and disillusioned as he finds himself no further on. The "To be or not to be" soliloquy is an example of doubt leading back to itself. Interestingly, the National Computer Centre found it a suitable subject for a simple flow diagram (Appendix 3) which admirably illustrates the circular, indecisive logic of the passage.

All this doubt possibly reflects the age of uncertainty in which Shakespeare lived. Peter Hall[5] supports this view:

> The darkest and most penetrating statement of the human condition, the play is the product of a time of doubt. The boundless vigour of the Renaissance was failing, and the glorious Elizabethan age was, like its monarch, in decline.

Interpreting HAMLET

At the very beginning of our survey of *Hamlet* (Page 2) we remarked that the play was capable of an infinite variety of interpretations. It is the first task of a director thinking his way towards a production to decide which facets of the play he wishes to display, since he cannot possibly highlight them all. The disadvantage of this is that each interpretation will have only a limited validity; but, on the other hand, each new interpretation will contribute further to our appreciation of the world's most fascinating drama.

Clearly the performance of *Hamlet* on the stage is of prime importance for our understanding of the play, for outside the theatre Shakespeare (*pace* Hazlitt) can have only an incomplete, emasculated existence. Therefore we shall later set aside a full chapter for the discussion of *Hamlet* in production.

---

[5] Peter Hall: *op cit.*

Chapter 3

Hamlet and Tragedy

Whatever Shakespeare had in mind as his total concept in writing *Hamlet*, we should be in danger of having a distorted view of the play if we were to forget that, first and foremost, it is a piece of theatre. T. S. Eliot*, even in criticizing *Hamlet* on artistic grounds, admits that it is an "interesting" play, and Dr Johnson praised it for its "variety". If there are scholarly problems of ambiguity and inconsistency, such as Hamlet's age or in Horatio's relationship with Hamlet (Page 66), they disappear in the illusion of the theatre: we are led unquestioningly along by the drama; our mood is moulded by the poetry and the vigour of the play's language (see Chapter 10).

IS *HAMLET* A MELODRAMA?

The excitement and interest of the play are typical of Elizabethan drama. We pointed out earlier (Page 6) that *Hamlet* lies in the tradition of the revenge tragedy, which was primarily melodramatic, and many of the scenes and incidents in the play ought perhaps to be interpreted with this fact in mind. But the straightforward purpose of melodrama is to thrill and intrigue, and if the melodramatist succeeds in thrilling and intriguing us, then that is the extent of his concern, whereas *Hamlet* goes much deeper than this. It seems to be concerned with some sort of values, with the relationship between man and the universe; it seems to be concerned with man's feelings and behaviour towards other men. These are the factors which make us value *Hamlet* as more than melodrama – as a tragedy.

Some aspects of HAMLET as a Tragedy

When A. C. Bradley* set out to elucidate the nature of Shakespearian tragedy, he had in mind as a yardstick the concept of Greek tragedy offered by Aristotle in the *Poetics*. Therefore he expected something on these lines: a tragedy is about a calamity, usually resulting in death, which has been brought on by some flaw or excess causing imbalance in the hero's make-up. Before his death, the hero is allowed to attain a better knowledge of himself and a fuller understanding of life. The sadness lies in the waste of life and prosperity (in its widest sense) which have been sacrificed to achieve this greater understanding. We, as the audience, must achieve a bond of sympathy and identification with the hero in his predicament.

THE FATAL FLAW[1]

The first point to consider, then, is the presence of this fatal flaw in the hero's character which will lead to the tragedy. There is, perhaps, a reference to this in the passage which is ostensibly about drunkenness in Denmark but which might be constructed as a more general description of the nature of a tragic flaw:

> So, oft it chances in particular men,   I 4 23
> That for some vicious mole of nature in them,
> As in their birth, wherein they are not guilty
> (Since nature cannot choose his origin),
> By the o'ergrowth of some complexion,
> Oft breaking down the pales and forts of reason,
> Or by some habit, that too much o'er-leavens
> The form of plausive manners – that these men,
> Carrying I say the stamp of one defect,
> Being nature's livery, or fortune's star,
> His virtues else be they as pure as grace,
> As infinite as man may undergo,
> Shall in the general censure take corruption
> From that particular fault: the dram of evil
> Doth all the noble substance of a doubt,
> To his own scandal.

Such a flaw of character bringing catastrophe can be found in other Shakespearian tragedies: Othello's jealousy and credulity bring him to the murder of Desdemona; Lear's vanity and lack of judgement lead directly to his degradation. But what does Hamlet do to bring about *his* tragic situation?

AN IMPOSED TRAGIC SITUATION

Here we must accept that Hamlet is different from Shakespeare's other tragic heroes in that they contribute to the creation of their own predicament, whereas Hamlet has his imposed upon him. Admittedly, once the prince is embroiled willy-nilly in his situation, his reluctant handling of it leads to the sense of waste which constitutes the tragedy; but Hamlet does not himself bring about the situation in the first place. Hamlet's tragedy is one of being faced by appalling facts, by having forced upon him an intolerable task which he dutifully but tragically performs.

HAMLET A SYMPATHETIC HERO?

The purpose of tragedy, according to Aristotle, is the catharsis of certain emotions, one of which is pity. The exact concept of catharsis, a medical

[1] See Appendix I page 130.

term meaning purgation, has been the cause of some controversy. But
what is certain is that it involves the dramatist's asking every spectator,
every reader, to sympathise

> with his hero, to feel with him, to place himself in his shoes, to understand his situation . . .

If we are alienated by Hamlet, if we feel irritated by him, like Marowitz, for example (Page 2), then there can be no tragedy.

Usually Hamlet's situation has been accepted with unadulterated sympathy. He has been described as too gentle a person to perform a harsh task: Goethe[2] speaks of him in these terms:

> a lovely, pure and most moral nature, without the strength of nerve which forms a hero, sinks beneath a burden which it cannot bear and must not cast away. (Page 39).

Dover Wilson* professes himself angry at what he calls "Goethe's condescending sentimentalism" and prefers to see Hamlet's predicament as

> a great and noble spirit subjected to a moral shock so overwhelming that it shatters all zest for life and all belief in it;

a different but equally sympathetic view (Page 40).

Not all critics, however, have written of Hamlet in completely sympathetic terms. Some have found that his harsh treatment of Ophelia in the "nunnery" scene and of Gertrude in the closet scene, the relish with which he reports to Horatio the death of Rosencrantz and Guildenstern, and his disgusting words about Polonius and the worms, are alienating. Hamlet is seen as cruel, his mind is poisonous; according to Wilson Knight*:

> In the universe of the play . . . he is the only discordant element, the only hindrance to happiness, health and prosperity; a living death in the midst of life. (cf. Claudius Page 61)

By presenting Hamlet in this way, "the poet divides our sympathies".

THE FINAL NOBILITY

Nevertheless, whatever our attitudes towards Hamlet during the course of the play, Shakespeare is careful to portray him at the end in such a way as to catch our sympathy for him. He accepts Laertes' challenge, about which he ought to have been very wary, with seeming carelessness, reminding us in doing so of Claudius's earlier tribute to him:

> . . . he being remiss   IV 7 133
> Most generous, and free from all contriving,
> Will not peruse the foils . . .

There is, too, a nobility in his request for forgiveness by Laertes before the fencing match (Page 54) and his own forgiveness *of* Laertes after the match.

---

[2] J. W. Goethe: *Wilhelm Meister's Apprenticeship* 1795 (Collier-Macmillan) 1962.

28 Fortinbras and Horatio, moreover, are given the task of setting the appropriate mood of sympathy for Hamlet as he dies. Horatio thinks so highly of his friend that he wishes to die with him, but Hamlet persuades him that a better course of action is to remain behind to mourn and to tell Hamlet's story truly:

> If thou didst ever hold me in thy heart   V 2 344
> Absent thee from felicity awhile,
> And in this harsh world draw thy breath in pain,
> To tell my story . . .

Horatio's panegyric to Hamlet is brief but strikes the right note:

> Now cracks a noble heart. Good night, sweet prince;   V 2 357
> And flights of angels sing thee to thy rest!

It is left to Fortinbras to create the final impression of Hamlet's nobility and the waste of potential caused by his death:

>   Let four captains   V 2 393
> Bear Hamlet like a soldier to the stage,
> For he was likely, had he been put on,
> To have proved most royal . . .

A RELIGIOUS PLAY?

Man not only needs to live with his own kind but also with the universe, with the gods or, in Christian terms, with God. In Greek tragedy, the universe is manifest in terms of Providence or Fate: we have the feeling that man must be careful not to assume too great an opinion of himself for he never knows when Providence will strike a blow at his happiness and prosperity. There is clearly something of this atmosphere in the situation imposed on Hamlet: evil has been introduced by events entirely outside his control and he has to attempt to mitigate its consequences. In pagan terms, there is no difficulty about the existence of evil in the world: it is an accepted part of the divine pattern. For a Christian, however, evil presents a less tractable problem. How can one square the presence of evil with an omnipotent and benevolent God?

Superficially, *Hamlet* can be construed as a Christian play in as much as it has a conventional framework. Hamlet talks of God and His condemnation of suicide; a ghost comes from Hell; a murderer prays to God for forgiveness; a supposed suicide is given a curtailed burial service, and the dying hero is commended to the care of God's angels. Indeed, Hamlet's reluctance to perform his task has been explained in Christian terms as an unwillingness to allow the end (the bringing of Claudius to justice) to justify the means (the killing of Claudius). In fact, however, the morality of the play is ambiguous, neither wholly Christian nor wholly pagan, which probably contributes to the uncertainty of Hamlet's reaction to his situation.

Whatever the nature of Providence in the play, Hamlet certainly struggles against its imposition on his life.

HAMLET ACHIEVES A GREATER UNDERSTANDING OF MAN'S PREDICAMENT

Perhaps the most important aspect of *Hamlet* as a tragedy is described in our definition above (Page 25) as a "fuller understanding of life". The Hamlet who broods bitterly through the earlier part of the play is different from the Hamlet who speaks nobly to Laertes before the fencing match; and the point of change can be marked quite precisely. It occurs during his absence from Denmark when he escapes the death planned for him by means of the fortunate incident of the sea-fight. The Hamlet who left for England was full of doubt, cynicism and self-reproach; the Hamlet who returns is more friendly and humorous, more gentle, less melancholy and less worried about how he ought to act.

Something has happened to change his attitude. Whereas before he struggled against the situation in which Providence had trapped him, now he has acquiesced, become reconciled to it; he has become more mature, has reached a clearer understanding of the nature of life. This acquiescence is shown in two passages in the final scene:

> Our indiscretion sometime serves us well   V 2 8
> When our deep plots do pall, and that should learn us
> There's a divinity that shapes our ends,
> Rough-hew them how we will

and:

> we defy augury. There is special providence in the fall   V 2 217
> of a sparrow. If it be now, 'tis not to come—if it be not
> to come, it will be now—if it be not now, yet it will
> come—the readiness is all. Since no man, of aught he
> leaves, knows what is't to leave betimes, let be.

Earlier (Page 6) we offered four suggestions for the meaning of *Hamlet*; each must be considered in the light of these passages.

1) REVENGE IS DETERMINED In chapter two we suggested that Hamlet struggles with his conscience about the fitness of his taking revenge (and in chapter four we shall discuss this more fully). Now Hamlet seems to have recognised that he is a part of a moral order too big to be directed: he must live in the world as it is, not as he would wish it to be. If he escapes from reality, the reality will not cease to exist. He therefore seems resigned to action:

> If his fitness speaks, mine is ready; now or whensoever, V 2 200
> provided I be so able as now . . .

and realises that there is not much time left for him to take action:

> It will be short, the interim is mine . . . V 2 73※

2) EVIL IS A NECESSARY PART OF LIFE If the play is concerned with the
problem of evil in the world, if Hamlet's shrinking from evil causes his
uncertain response to his situation, then these passages show his acceptance
of the fact that

> evil is a necessary part of God's harmonious order, that man must live with
> evil while he opposes it as best he can. He must learn that death is the inevitable
> end of all, and he must learn that to achieve justice he must make of himself
> a passive instrument in the hands of God in the faith that God will preserve a
> just and benevolent moral order regardless of man's own feeble efforts. When
> Hamlet becomes impervious to the blows of fortune his mission will be
> accomplished. [3]

In the words of Blake:

> Man was made for Joy and Woe,
> And when this we rightly know
> Thro' the world we safely go.

3) DEATH IS TO BE ACCEPTED If the play is about death, if Hamlet's fear
is of the negation which is death, then these passages show that Hamlet
accepts the necessity and inevitability of death and that "the readiness is
all". He conquers his fear of the unknown futurity, reflecting perhaps a
similar moment in *King Lear* when Edgar says:

> Men must endure
> Their going hence, even as their coming here.
> Ripeness is all.

4) DOUBT IS DISPELLED. If the play is about "not knowing for sure"; if Hamlet
is a man, or indeed Everyman, who has lost his way, these passages indicate
that he has found it again.

AN OPTIMISTIC PLAY?

There is usually a feeling at the end of Shakespeare's tragedies that,
despite the torments, the degradation, the waste which has been presented,
everything has been worthwhile; a feeling that, despite his pettiness, his
weakness, his selfishness, man is somehow ennobled by the experience he

[3] Irving Ribner: *Patterns in Shakespearian Tragedy* (Methuen) 1970.

has undergone. In a word, Shakespearian tragedy ends on an optimistic note.

This is the accepted way of regarding the close of *Hamlet*. Evil has been purged and if the cost has been high, the exercise has been a success. The hero leaves us with an impression of his nobility (Page 27) and Fortinbras remains as the white hope of the future.

Not everyone is content with this view. Some directors feel that the introduction of Fortinbras right at the end of the play is inappropriate to the overall tone, that the presence of singing angels is artificial and sentimental and that it would have been more congruous for Shakespeare to have left us to deliberate the waste of it all with Hamlet's own remark: "the rest is silence". One such director, Peter Hall[4], writes:

> I don't find *Hamlet* a tragedy in the sense that at the end of it I am left ennobled, purged and regenerated. I think it belongs with *Measure for Measure* as a clinical dissection of life. It is a shattering play, a worrying play.

[4] Peter Hall: *op cit.*

Chapter 4

A Question of Delay

For many critics the most important question to be asked about Hamlet is why he delays in executing his revenge.

It has been maintained that, in fact, Hamlet does not delay at all but kills Claudius as early in the play as is materially possible, in the true spirit of the revenge tragedy (Page 6).

INDICATIONS OF DELAY

Such a theory can be made to sound very plausible, but its validity is thrown open to doubt by several factors:

Firstly, there is an intended contrast between Hamlet and Laertes which gives it the lie (Page 64).

Secondly, the comic scenes in Shakespeare's plays, apart from their obvious entertainment value, usually have further significance as a commentary on the main action. So in V I the chatter of the grave-diggers contains, in the nonsensical, unprogressive logic of the first clown, a satire on Hamlet's inability to act:

> It argues an act, and an act hath three branches: V I II
> it is to act, to do and to perform.

Thirdly, in his tragedies Shakespeare usually hints at the nature of the themes in the play by means of certain oblique passages; i.e. passages which superficially are about one thing but in undertone suggest another. In *Hamlet* these oblique passages seem to refer to delay and the fading of resolution and are as follows:-

a) The soliloquy beginning "To be or not to be" is usually regarded as Hamlet's consideration, philosophically rather than emotionally, of the unsatisfactory nature of man's life on earth and the possibilities which death offers as a means of escape from life's problems. (Page 19). He rejects the notion of leaving life because of the uncertainty of what would follow death (Page 21). Whatever the immediate subject of the soliloquy, its overall imaginative atmosphere is one of loss of purpose and direction:

> Thus conscience does make cowards of us all,   III I 83
> And thus the native hue of resolution

Is sicklied o'er with the pale cast of thought,
And enterprises of great pitch and moment
With this regard their currents turn awry,
And lose the name of action.

In these lines Hamlet is consciously or unconsciously referring to his own condition regarding his vengeance on Claudius.

b) The advice which ironically Claudius offers to Laertes might more logically have been applied to Hamlet, and Shakespeare surely intended his audience to realise this:

That we would do   IV 7 117
We should do when we would: for this 'would' changes,
And hath abatements and delays as many
As there are tongues, are hands, are accidents,
And then this 'should' is like a spendthrift sigh,
That hurts by easing.

EVIDENCE OF DELAY IN THE TEXT

More directly, from a consideration of the text of the play it would seem that Hamlet is guilty of delay and, what is more, considering himself guilty, tries to discover what it is that is preventing him from carrying out his revenge.

Certainly, in the moment of emotional stress brought on by the proximity of the ghost and the nature of its revelation, Hamlet expresses a clear intent to exact revenge quickly:

Haste me to know't, that I with wings as swift   I 5 29
As meditation or the thoughts of love,
May sweep to my revenge.

He promises in the most emphatic language to keep his quest for vengeance always at the front of his mind:

Remember thee?   I 5 95
Ay thou poor ghost whiles memory holds a seat
In this distracted globe.

On the spur of the moment Hamlet seems committed to, even enthusiastic about, the task set before him. Yet by the end of the same scene he is already beginning to have regrets:

The time is out of joint, O cursèd spite,   I 5 188
That ever I was born to set it right!

34 When we meet Hamlet again, two months have passed between Acts I and II. During this time, the prince has created some impression on his surroundings because of his mental state (Page 52) but he has made no effort to further his revenge. It is perhaps wrong to literalise the time lag at this point. Inside the play, dramatic time rather than actual time must be allowed to prevail, and it is unlikely that a theatre audience would notice the mathematical calculations needed to establish the two month gap; they would not be aware of any great passage of time.

HAMLET FEELS GUILTY OF DELAY AND REBUKES HIMSELF. Nevertheless, Hamlet already feels a sense of guilt that his protestations to the ghost have not yet been realised. He is moved, by the passion of the player's speech, to upbraid himself for his failure, in the soliloquy beginning:

see p31

> O, what a rogue and peasant slave am I! II 2 553

[The use of the soliloquy is very important in this play. It is the audience's equivalent of being allowed into Hamlet's thoughts. Thinking "aloud", he has no need to dissemble, and it is therefore safe to assume that in the soliloquies we have a true picture of the state of his mind *in so far as he himself is aware of it*. The soliloquy precludes pretence designed to deceive others but offers no guarantee against self-deception. It is interesting to note the frequency and length of the soliloquies in *Hamlet,* indicating the hero's loneliness and isolation. Perhaps only in the soliloquies and in his conversations with Horatio do we see a sincere Hamlet; at no other time can we be sure that he is not putting on an act of some kind. (Page 46 – the antic disposition)] Hamlet compares the intensity of the player's simulated passion with his own lack of feeling in a real situation:

> What's Hecuba to him, or he to Hecuba, II 2 562
> That he should weep for her? what would he do,
> Had he the motive and the cue for passion
> That I have?

In contrast, Hamlet calls himself a "dull and muddy-mettled rascal". He tries to find a reason for his inadequacy: is he a coward? Perhaps he has some physical deficiency: a lack of the gall fluid which was thought to be the stimulant to bitter thoughts:

> it cannot be II 2 579
> But I am pigeon-livered, and lack gall
> To make oppression bitter, or ere this
> I should ha'fatted all the region kites
> With this slave's offal.

Stung by self-reproach, he relieves his feelings by hysterically cursing Claudius, a futile substitute for action:

> Bloody, bawdy villain!   II 2 583
> Remorseless, treacherous, lecherous, kindless villain!
> O, vengeance!

The language is reminiscent of that which Hamlet used to describe Claudius at the moment of the ghost's revelation, perhaps an indication that no progress has been made.

[It is worthwhile examining Hamlet's self-accusation of cowardice as the reason for delay. It is a reason which occurs to him two or three times in a slightly different form. We ought to consider Hamlet's behaviour throughout the play and decide whether he deserves the title of coward].

THE PLAY SCENE A DELAYING TACTIC? Eventually, Hamlet realises the pointlessness of his outburst and, thinking more calmly, produces the idea of the play-within-the-play:

> I'll have these players   II 2 598
> Play something like the murder of my father
> Before mine uncle. . .

Its purpose? To expose Claudius's guilt. The reason why this is necessary? Not, as is suggested by those who believe that Hamlet does not delay (Page 32), to make the king's guilt public, but to assure Hamlet himself of the guilt. Hamlet is now in some doubt about the genuineness of the ghost and its message:

> The spirit that I have seen   II 2 602
> May be a devil . . .

He must be sure:

> I'll have grounds   II 2 607
> More relative than this — the play's the thing
> Wherein I'll catch the conscience of the king.

The question for us is whether Hamlet could have a sincere doubt and therefore need reassurance, or whether the play is a mere device for procrastination. Certainly Hamlet was convinced of the genuineness of the ghost at the time of its appearance:

> Touching this vision here   I 5 137
> It is an honest ghost that let me tell you . . .

Whether he can now be genuinely less sure depends on the nature of the ghost (Page 66).

Ernest Jones* thought of the play-within-the-play as a substitute for action, a sort of intellectual revenge:

> Hamlet eagerly seizes at every excuse for occupying himself with any other matter than the performance of his duty: just as, on a lesser plane, a person faced with a distasteful task, e.g. writing a difficult letter, will whittle away his time in arranging, tidying and fidgeting with any little occupation that may serve as a pretext for procrastination.

The relevance of the soliloquy ("To be or not to be") to Hamlet's delay has already been indicated on Page 32. Notice again, however, the self-imputation of cowardice in

Thus conscience does make cowards of us all.   III 1 84

The play-within-the-play is a success: Claudius has been "frighted with false fire" and Hamlet is ecstatic. But does

I'll take the ghost's word for a thousand pounds   III 2 287

mark any real progress from

It is an honest ghost, that let me tell you?   I 5 138

Hamlet concludes III 2 with a protestation that, in the light of this new assurance,

now could I drink hot blood,   III 2 393
And do such bitter business as the day
Would quake to look on.

He seems determined at last to exact his revenge, yet when, a few moments later, he is presented with the perfect opportunity to do so, he rejects it.

THE PRAYER SCENE. The prayer scene has been the centre of much disagreement. Does perhaps Hamlet's opening phrase, "Now *might* I do it pat" rather than "will" or "can", indicate a lack of real conviction of intent? What is the reason for sparing Claudius? Hamlet says that, if the king dies at prayer, he will go to heaven, and this is to do him a favour rather than be revenged on him. Some critics regard Hamlet here as noble for not stabbing a kneeling, defenceless man, although such moral scruples are difficult to reconcile with the hatred which prefers to send Claudius straight to the torments of hell. Whatever the real reason for Hamlet's restraint, his ostensible reasons are shown to be unfounded; the king would have gone to hell had he been killed on this occasion; he has not achieved forgiveness:

[It is worth noting that from the end of the play scene Hamlet's delay becomes positively dangerous because, although he is now certain of Claudius's guilt, the king is equally aware of Hamlet's knowledge. Dramatically speaking, Hamlet's delay serves to intensify the action of the play and it is therefore as well to keep before us the simple fact that Hamlet's failure to kill Claudius in the prayer scene is theatrically necessary since it leads on to the deaths of Polonius, Ophelia, Rosencrantz and Guildenstern, Laertes, the Queen and Hamlet himself. Our immediate instinct might be to wish that he had acted more quickly, but that would be too simple: if we are to judge from Laertes' experience, precipitate action meets with no more success (Page 63).]

IN THE QUEEN'S CLOSET. Hamlet rails against the queen: he seems to find in the use of violent language a relief from and a substitute for his frustrating inability to act (Page 34).

In this scene Hamlet kills Polonius in a fit of action without time for consideration; an indication, perhaps, that it can only be in such a way that he will manage to dispose of Claudius (Page 35). Clearly, the stabbing of Polonius is intended to stand in stark contrast to the sparing of Claudius in the previous scene. What are we to make of it? Hamlet suggests that he has mistaken Polonius for Claudius. At the very moment of the thrust he asks

    Is it the king?   III 4 25

and a little later says

    I took thee for thy better . . .   III 4 32

If so, even more doubt is thrown on the sincerity of Hamlet's logic in the prayer scene since, if the king was in the state of grace necessary for heaven at that time, he surely still is. *— he's not praying now !!*

Hamlet's verbal assault on Gertrude is interrupted by the appearance of the ghost. Hamlet's first words to it are significant:

    Do you not come your tardy son to chide,   III 4 106
    That lapsed in time and passion lets go by
    Th'important acting of your dread command?

Hamlet feels guilty of delay, and the ghost confirms that he *has* delayed:

    Do not forget! this visitation   III 4 110
    Is but to whet thy almost blunted purpose.

A QUESTION OF DELAY

38

It is possible to explain Hamlet's erratic behaviour by regarding it as a manifestation of his uncertainty: revenge is a convention but, for Hamlet, the conventional gesture would be meaningless. Perhaps he needs to persuade himself of the necessity and justice of acting; he must act thinkingly, not merely as "passion's slave."

MORE SELF-REBUKE. In the soliloquy occasioned by the passing of Fortinbras's army, Hamlet again laments his failure to act. As in the soliloquy following the player's passionate speech, Hamlet compares himself unfavourably with these soldiers who are marching to engage in great action with little cause whilst he with great cause produces little action (but see Page 64). He refers, in a phrase reminiscent of the ghost's last speech, to his "dull revenge" (dull—blunted). Again he seeks for reasons for his delay. Is it "bestial oblivion", the forgetfulness of duty which the ghost referred to? Or is it

> some craven scruple IV 4 40
> Of thinking too precisely on th'event –
> A thought which quartered hath but one part wisdom,
> And ever three parts coward:

too much weighing of the pros and cons so that the desire to act falters and loses momentum? Certainly the "thinking too precisely" fits the prayer scene and strongly recalls the "To be or not to be" soliloquy with the same imputation of moral cowardice (Page 36).

After considering these possibilities, Hamlet admits his own puzzlement:

> I do not know IV 4 43
> Why yet I live to say 'This thing's to do',
> Sith I have cause, and will, and strength, and means,
> To do't . . .

The words which close the soliloquy:

> O, from this time forth IV 4 65
> My thoughts be bloody, or be nothing worth!

recall the earlier:

> now could I drink hot blood . . . III 2 393

but we might feel disinclined to believe him because he has so devalued the currency of his protestations.

REVENGE AT LAST! Eventually, Hamlet does kill Claudius, although by now it is revenge not only for Old Hamlet but for himself and Gertrude and the others who have been victims of the consequences of the king's crime. On this occasion, as with the murder of Polonius, Hamlet, with "not half an hour of life", has no time for thinking "too precisely". He is finally forced into immediate but long-delayed action.

Some Suggestions why Hamlet Delays

Hamlet, then, delays but is uncertain of the cause of his doing so. The critics, by contrast, have often been boldly assertive in their attempts to pluck out the heart of Hamlet's mystery although they have been unable to find much common ground.

Admittedly, one group has taken the view that we can never really come to know why Hamlet delays. Ernest Jones suggests that the reasons for his inability to exact revenge are seated so deeply in his subconscious that he does not even know himself the cause of his failure. John Lawlor[1] remarks:

> Hamlet gives us *reasons* enough for delay, *causes* none; for the cause remains unknown to him, and to us.

Professor Muir[2] considers this impossibility of identifying these causes to be an intentional part of the play's design:

> *Hamlet* is a play about the mystery and impenetrability of human personality.

The opinions of other critics fall into three broad categories:

1) HAMLET IS NOT FITTED FOR THE TASK

Is there something in Hamlet's own nature which hinders him from acting? Goethe described Hamlet in these terms:

> a lovely, pure, noble and most moral nature, without the strength of nerve which forms a hero, sinks beneath a burden which it cannot bear and must not cast away.

Goethe's Hamlet is a weak, gentle, retiring man to whom violence is distasteful. A. C. Bradley* refuted this "sentimental" view of Hamlet by pointing to the various incidents in the play where the hero behaves in quite robust fashion: the breaking away from Horatio fearlessly to follow the ghost; the speaking daggers to Gertrude; the despatching of Polonius and, later, Rosencrantz and Guildenstern without undue remorse; and the wrestling with Laertes at Ophelia's graveside.

Sometimes criticism of Goethe's type has become fogged by a too-close identification of the critic with the character. Thus Coleridge, an over-reflective intellectual, diagnosed over-reflective intellectualism as the cause of Hamlet's delay, whilst Schopenhauer, a world-weary cynic, diagnosed world-weary cynicism. Coleridge wrote, significantly: "I have a smack of Hamlet myself, if I may say so".

---

[1] John Lawlor: *The Tragic Sense in Shakespeare* (Chatto and Windus) 1960.
[2] K. Muir: 'Shakespeare and the Tragic Pattern' *Proceedings of the British Academy* XLIV 1958.

2) REVENGE IS AGAINST HIS PRINCIPLES.

Is the task of revenge repugnant to Hamlet? John Lawlor wrote[3]:

> This, I submit, is the tragic conflict in *Hamlet;* the hero averse from the deed
> that is required of him, seeking endlessly the cause of his aversion, calling it
> by any name but its own, and failing to know it for what it is.

Although in an earlier code of behaviour the duty of revenge would be clear, for Hamlet the ethics of vengeance are questionable. Early in the play he says:

> The time is out of joint; O cursèd spite,   I 5 188
> That ever I was born to set it right. . . .

and even as late as Act V he still seems to be debating the morality of taking revenge when he asks Horatio

>   is't not perfect conscience   V 2 67
> To quit him with this arm? and is't not to be damned,
> To let this canker of our nature come
> In further evil?

Perhaps Hamlet is in doubt because he lives in an age of doubt (Page 23). Harley Granville-Barker* says:

> Hamlet is a man adrift from old faiths and not yet anchored in new; a man
> of his time in that more particularly, the typical hero in a new age of doubt.

3) HE IS TOO DISILLUSIONED TO ACT

Is Hamlet so deeply disillusioned by life that the will to act is stifled and apathetic melancholy results? Wilson Knight* writes:

> He does not avenge his father's death, not because he dare not, not because
> he hates the thought of bloodshed, but because his "wit's diseased" (Page 49);
> his will is snapped and useless, like a broken leg. Nothing is worthwhile.

L. C. Knights* thought that Hamlet could not escape from a numbing sense of the meaninglessness of life in the corrupt environment of Denmark. What paralyses him is an overwhelming sense of evil. The effect of evil upon Hamlet is one way of considering the play as a dramatic entity (Page 11).

All these views about delay treat Hamlet sympathetically as indeed they must do if Hamlet is to be considered a tragic hero. If Hamlet irritates and alienates us totally, as he obviously does Marowitz, (Page 2), the purity of our response to the tragedy will be affected (Page 26).

---

[3] John Lawlor: *op cit.*

Chapter 5

Hamlet and his Mother

If disillusionment by the evil present in Denmark is the cause of Hamlet's apathetic delay, then one aspect of that evil is worthy of special consideration: Gertrude. Perhaps an examination of Hamlet's relationship to his mother can help to shed light on the mystery of the prince.

A. J. A. Waldock* sees the mother-son relationship as central to any understanding of the play. He begins by asking: "What is Hamlet most concerned about?" and answers that his greatest preoccupation is with his mother. He can be accused of forgetting his duty of vengeance, but he never forgets how his mother has behaved. Only a few lines after Hamlet has promised the ghost that he will "wipe away all trivial fond records" from his brain and leave room only for thoughts of revenge, his mind turns involuntarily back to that "most pernicious woman" (I 5 105).

In the first soliloquy, Hamlet is already deeply distressed *before* the ghost's revelation. His world has turned rotten:

> How weary, stale, flat and unprofitable   I 2 133
> Seem to me all the uses of this world!
> Fie on't, ah fie, 'tis an unweeded garden
> That grows to seed, things rank and gross in nature
> Possess it merely.

And the reason for this depression is Gertrude's early remarriage.

GERTRUDE'S EARLY REMARRIAGE HAS EMBITTERED HAMLET

The depth of Hamlet's passion in this soliloquy cannot be doubted: it is expressed both in the disjointed sentences (as if his mind is too troubled to think smoothly or as if he does not want to believe what he is saying – "Let me not think on't"), and in the content of the passage – mention of suicide, the feeling that his whole being is "sullied", tainted by his mother's incest. In fact the remarriage is a strong aspect of the corrupt background of the play, and Hamlet sees himself as fleshly related to the corruption personified in Claudius – "man and wife is one flesh". Dover Wilson* says that we cannot make too much of this incest-business: he points to its position in the forefront of the play and to the power with which it is introduced in this soliloquy. He sees the play as the experience of a great and noble spirit subjected to a moral shock (the remarriage) so over-whelming that it shatters all zest for life and all belief in it.

Certainly there is evidence that the shock of his mother's remarriage has warped Hamlet's responses. Because of this one woman's inconstancy, all womankind must be similarly unfaithful:

> . . . frailty, thy name is woman!   I 2 146

[This generalisation includes Ophelia and might go some way towards elucidating the problem of the Hamlet/Ophelia relationship (Page 55).]

There is a world of cynicism in the conversation with Horatio:

> Hamlet: But what is your affair in Elsinore?   I 2 174
>   We'll teach you to drink deep ere you depart.
> Horatio: My lord, I came to see your father's funeral.
> Hamlet: I prithee do not mock me fellow-student;
>   I think it was to see my mother's wedding.
> Horatio: Indeed, my lord, it followed hard upon.
> Hamlet: Thrift, thrift, Horatio, the funeral baked meats
>   Did coldly furnish forth the marriage tables.

Furthermore, Hamlet is preoccupied throughout the play, especially in the dialogue with Ophelia, with fidelity and chastity. Ophelia's statement to Hamlet in the play scene, "You are merry", brings the prompt rejoinder:

> What should a man do but be merry, for look you how   III 2 123
> cheerfully my mother looks, and my father died
> within's two hours.

The very word "mother" becomes an instrument of self-torture for Hamlet: he plays on it:

> We shall obey were she ten times our mother   III 2 334

and

> My mother – father and mother is man and wife; man   IV 3 50
> and wife is one flesh, and so, my mother.

The climax of all this brooding bitterness is reached in the scene in Gertrude's room where Hamlet gives vent to his tormented spirit. The dark thoughts and images which pour forth are an indication of the agitation of Hamlet's mind:

>   Nay, but to live   III 4 92
> In the rank sweat of an enseaméd bed
> Stewed in corruption, honeying, and making love
> Over the nasty sty.

The obvious disgust of the imagery at this point has led to suggestions that Hamlet suffers from what we now call an Oedipus complex. Certainly, he approaches hysteria as he speaks of the sexual act between Gertrude and Claudius, and despite Gertrude's pleas he will not relinquish the subject until the ghost intervenes.

Two questions occur to us about Gertrude:

a) Did she and Claudius commit adultery before the murder of Old Hamlet? The answer to this lies in the ghost's speech: he calls Claudius "that adulterate beast" (I 5 42) who won Gertrude to "his shameful lust", and Gertrude herself is "my most *seeming*-virtuous queen." The indications are that they did. Really, however, there is no need to consider the adultery in physical terms: marriage with a dead brother's widow would be classed as adultery by the ecclesiastical laws of the time. Witness the problems Henry VIII had!

b) Was she implicated in the murder of Old Hamlet? Did she have knowledge of it? Her astonishment at Hamlet's comment on Polonius's death would seem to exonerate her:

> Queen: O what a rash and bloody deed is this!   III 4 27
> Hamlet: A bloody deed – almost as bad, good mother,
> As kill a king, and marry with his brother.
> Queen: As kill a king!

On the whole the critics have been disposed to treat Gertrude kindly. Wilson Knight considered that Hamlet's vile abuse of his mother served to alienate him from our sympathy. A. C. Bradley* thought her naive:

> The queen was not a bad-hearted woman . . . But she had a soft animal nature, and was very dull and very shallow. She loved to be happy, like a sheep in the sun; and, to do her justice, it pleased her to see others happy.

Bradley's point is valid. Gertrude's simple way of looking at things is shown by her romantic words at the burial of Ophelia:

> Sweets to the sweet. Farewell!   V 1 237
> I hoped thou shouldst have been my Hamlet's wife:
> I thought thy bride-bed to have decked, sweet maid,
> And not have strewed thy grave.

How sweetly superficial! Again, she fails to understand the depths of Hamlet's feelings and assumes with her

> Good Hamlet, cast thy nighted colour off   I 2 68

that the simple answer to her son's problems is a stiff upper lip and a few therapeutic sets at tennis. Further, when Hamlet makes Gertrude face the reality of her position, her reaction

Thou turn'st my eyes into my very soul,   III 4 89

and the ghost's description:

amazement on thy mother sits,   III 4 112

suggest a kind of silly innocence.

H. D. F. Kitto[1] saw her as a tragic figure unwittingly overwhelmed by the consequences of her sin:

> After her own sin, and as a direct consequence of it, everything that she holds dear is blasted.

T. S. ELIOT CALLED THE PLAY "AN ARTISTIC FAILURE".

It was a consideration of the Hamlet/Gertrude relationship which caused T. S. Eliot* to declare *Hamlet* "an artistic failure". Like A. J. A. Waldock, Eliot felt that the main business of the play is the effect of Gertrude's action on Hamlet. He agreed that Hamlet is dominated by a strong disgust and disillusionment springing from that action, but in terms of the play Gertrude is not an adequate equivalent for the depths of that disgust. (Certainly, she does not herself present a strong character in the play; it needs careful direction to make much of her). Shakespeare's other tragedies have an artistic inevitability which lies in a just proportion between the external agent and the emotion generated by that agent. Thus, in *Othello*, Iago is portrayed as being so cunning that Othello *inevitably* becomes entangled in his web; in *Antony and Cleopatra*, Cleopatra is so fascinating that it is *inevitable* that Antony should throw away the Roman Empire for her. *Hamlet* lacks this inevitability. Gertrude's part in the play (i.e. her character) is not such that it would provoke Hamlet's reaction, and it must follow that Hamlet cannot understand his feelings because, in terms of the play, he cannot justify them; therefore they remain to poison life and obstruct action.

Eliot does admit, however, that it is possible for sensitive people to experience emotions in excess of their cause, but hints at some instability in this state of mind:

> The intense feeling, ecstatic or terrible, without an object or exceeding its object, is something which every person of sensibility has known. It often occurs in adolescence.

Rather interestingly, Laforgue, one of the strongest formative influences on Eliot's own poetry, saw Hamlet's behaviour as that of an adolescent whose central motivating force was a desire to escape from the complexities of adult life.

[1] H. D. F. Kitto: *op cit.*

Eliot concludes that Shakespeare was unable successfully to impose this motive (the effect of the mother's guilt) upon the "intractable" material of the old play (*the Ur-Hamlet*). Hence, the play is an artistic failure.

Dover Wilson* argues strongly against Eliot's view. We should concentrate, not on Gertrude herself, but on the "hideous thought of incest". Quite apart from any feelings which might be generated by Gertrude, the mere thought of the incestuous union between a man and his dead brother's wife would have been nauseous to a 17th century audience. He concludes:

> Given Hamlet's youth and the nobility of spirit which the [first] soliloquy reveals (Page 41); given the imagination of a great poet, which no one will deny [Hamlet]; given the fact of incest and the revelation of the Ghost, and given the "sore distraction" which disgust and horror bring in their train, what facts external to the play do we need to explain his behaviour to Ophelia and his mother, or to account for his inaction?

Dover Wilson, then, finds Hamlet's conduct perfectly explicable but, he adds, not necessarily excusable. (Page 53)

Chapter 6

Hamlet's State of Mind

It is sometimes difficult to distinguish between cause and effect in Hamlet, and nowhere is this more the case than in the problem of his "madness"

The "Antic Disposition."

ADOPTED TO *DIVERT* SUSPICION . . .

In the sources from which Shakespeare derived *Hamlet*, the hero feigns madness in order to divert suspicion while he gets on with plotting his revenge (Page 3), a device which would have been readily acceptable to Shakespeare's audience as a commonplace of the contemporary theatre: Edgar in *King Lear* assumes the part of a crazed beggarman by way of disguise, and Flamineo in Webster's *The White Devil* (first performed in 1608 and therefore about eight years later than *Hamlet*) says:

> I will feign a mad humour for the disgrace of my
> sister, and that will keep off idle questions.

Something of this is present in Shakespeare's play: after the ghost's revelation, Hamlet indicates that he

> perchance hereafter shall think meet I 5 171
> To put an antic disposition on.

Some passages in the play are fairly clear examples of Hamlet's adoption of this "antic disposition":

a) Hamlet's conversation with Polonius is apparently illogical but has hidden meanings: "fishmonger" (II 2 174) is an Elizabethan slang term for "bawd" so that Hamlet is commenting cryptically upon Polonius' using of Ophelia (Page 13).

At this stage, Polonius is convinced that the cause of Hamlet's "distemper" is his rejection by Ophelia and he is probing Hamlet. Unfortunately for him, Hamlet is well aware of the situation and by harping on the word "daughter" he leads Polonius by the nose.

Hamlet concludes his 'disjointed' conversation with a viciously satirical picture of an old man, and even Polonius becomes dimly aware that he is being toyed with. "Though this be madness, yet there is method in't" (II 2 206) he says, with more irony than he knows.

Hamlet gives the final proof that his gibberish is designed to dupe Polonius by his aside:

These tedious old fools!

b) Later in the scene, Hamlet again fools Polonius by the same trick (II 2 412) of pretending not to recognise him but talking about daughters.

c) At the beginning of the play-scene, Hamlet leaves Horatio with the words:

They're coming to the play. I must be idle,   III 2 89

where "be idle" means "assume my antic disposition and play the fool". Like Polonius in the earlier scenes, Claudius can make nothing of Hamlet's ensuing dialogue, although it obviously worries him.

Dr. Johnson remarked that in the performances of his day Hamlet's madness caused "much mirth", and certainly the Elizabethans derived some fun not only from their stage madmen but also from the genuinely mad, whom they regarded as objects of laughter. There is an element of black comedy in all the Elizabethan/Jacobean portrayals of madness; for example, in Webster's *The White Devil* and *The Duchess of Malfi* and Shakespeare's *King Lear* and, of course, *Hamlet*. The modern trend is to play Hamlet as an entirely serious part. Perhaps we have lost something!

. . . IN FACT HELPS TO *GENERATE* SUSPICION

This assumed "antic disposition", Claudius's attempts to sift its meaning and Hamlet's evasion of those attempts form the main interest of the second act; for, although the original purpose of feigning madness in the source was to divert suspicion, Hamlet's behaviour in Shakespeare's play soon makes Claudius very suspicious indeed:

a) Even before Hamlet's visit to Ophelia's closet has been reported to Claudius, the king has sent for Rosencrantz and Guildenstern to spy on Hamlet and discover the cause of his "transformation" (II 2).

b) At the beginning of III 4 Claudius is anxious about Hamlet's

turbulent and dangerous lunacy.   III 1 4

Rosencrantz and Guildenstern have been foxed by Hamlet: they have succeeded in getting him to admit that "he feels himself distracted" but he will not say why. He cannot give them a "wholesome answer" to their questions, he says, because his "wit's diseased", a sure sign that he is playing them up.

They have noticed that he

> with a crafty madness keeps aloof
> When we would bring him on to some confession
> Of his true state.

III 1 8

c) After the "nunnery" episode (Page 53), the king is inclined to agree with Rosencrantz and Guildenstern: Hamlet's madness does not stem from rejection by Ophelia, but is a meaningful and ominous condition:

> Love! his affections do not that way tend,   III 1 165
> Nor what he spake, though it lacked form a little,
> Was not like madness.

He is now fully alert to the dangers and decides that Hamlet must be removed to England:

> Madness in great ones must not unwatched go.   III 1 193

d) The play scene convinces Claudius that Hamlet is dangerous:

> nor stands it safe with us   III 3 1
> To let his madness range.

In fact, Hamlet, having taken the trouble to assume the "antic disposition", seems not to care whether Claudius suspects him or not. Rather, as the play progresses, he seems almost to welcome the king's knowledge of the position, as if he wanted a confrontation (Page 59):

a) He tells Claudius's spies

> I am but mad north-north-west,   II 2 382

implying that for most of the time he has all his wits about him. Rosencrantz and Guildenstern duly report back to Claudius their opinion of Hamlet's "crafty madness".

b) But he urges Gertrude not to tell Claudius

> That I essentially am not in madness,   III 4 187
> But mad in craft.

A SAFETY VALVE?

Apart from the source reason of averting suspicion, Shakespeare may have had more subtle reasons in mind for making Hamlet assume his "antic disposition". John Dover Wilson* looks at the moment when Hamlet makes his decision to do so (I 5 171). He points out that in the hundred lines which precede that decision Hamlet is in

UNDERSTANDING HAMLET

a state of extreme emotional instability, and with an intellect tottering on its seat.

We are to feel, therefore, that he assumes madness because he cannot retain perfect control over himself. The "antic disposition" will act as a sort of outlet, enabling him "to give some utterance to the load that pressed on his heart and brain", as A. C. Bradley* put it.

This further use of the assumed madness is an indication of Shakespeare's improvement on crude source material, for undoubtedly the device blurs into Hamlet's own character. George Rylands wrote:

> Amleth of history feigned a foolish and grotesque madness and under his mad speech concealed an unfathomable cunning, mingling craft and candour. Thus, our Hamlet's madness, over which critics and doctors have spilt so much ink, was taken over by Shakespeare as part of the conception. It was a genuine pretence. Shakespeare improves on this, sees deeper into it and naturalizes it, making it indeed a safety-valve for the prince's melancholy and hysteria.

This blending of the two strains of assumed madness and a genuine instability is the cause of the problem. Significantly, A. J. A. Waldock* feels that Shakespeare does not marry them successfully.

"Sore Distraction"

Hamlet's sensitive nature has suffered two crushing blows: Gertrude's early remarriage and the Ghost's revelation. Who can be surprised that all this has knocked him off balance? It is interesting to note Polonius's catalogue of the progress of Hamlet's mental state during the two months that have passed since the prince became fully aware of his father's murder: Hamlet

> Fell into a sadness, then into a fast,   II 2 147
> Thence to a watch, thence into a weakness,
> Thence to a lightness, and by this declension,
> Into the madness wherein now he raves.

This speech is usually dismissed as yet another example of Polonius's verbosity but perhaps, considering its position, we could look on it as Shakespeare telling us how far Hamlet has declined since we last saw him.

HAMLET DISILLUSIONED

Hamlet, as we meet him in Act II, has lost all his "mirth". His mind is poisoned, he has "bad dreams"; and these manifest themselves in his morbidity, his preoccupation with death (Page 22), and in his general cynicism:

a) The whole earth seems foul to him:

it goes so heavily with my disposition, that this goodly   II 2 301
frame the earth, seems to me a sterile promontory,
this most excellent canopy the air, look you, this
grave o'er hanging firmament, this majestical roof
fretted with golden fire, why it appeareth nothing
to me but a foul and pestilent congregation of vapours.

and

How weary, stale, flat and unprofitable,   I 3 133
Seem to me all the uses of this world!
Fie on't, ah fie, 'tis an unweeded garden
That grows to seed, things rank and gross in nature
Possess it merely.

b) Man delights him not. He denies the whole tenor of Renaissance
optimism about the innate nobility of man, a being just one step below the
angels:

What a piece of work is a man, how noble in reason,   II 2 307
how infinite in faculties, in form and moving, how
express and admirable in action, how like an angel in
apprehension, how like a god: the beauty of the world;
the paragon of animals; and yet to me, what is this
quintessence of dust? man delights not me,

and

To be honest as this world goes, is to be one man   II 2 178
picked out of ten thousand,

and

Use every man after his desert, and who shall 'scape   II 2 533
whipping?

c) His mind dwells constantly on the foulest aspects of life and his brain is
fertile in its ability to create repellent images. He talks of the sun breeding
maggots in a dead dog; he describes old age in the most unpleasant way –

Old men have grey beards, . . . their faces are wrinkled,   II 2 198
their eyes purging thick amber and plum-tree gum,
and . . . they have a plentiful lack of wit, together with
most weak hams (Page 46).

He is fascinated by decay and putrescence: in the dialogue about dead Polonius, who is at supper "where a' is eaten – a certain convocation of politic worms are e'en at him" (IV 3 19); and in the graveyard scene where he is admonished by Horatio for considering "too curiously" (V 1 200).

INSTABILITY

The distracted state of Hamlet's mind shows itself in another way: in the form of an instability characterized by violent changes of mood:

a) In the 'cellerage' scene where his excited state provokes Horatio's comment about "wild and whirling words" (I 5 135) (Page 35).

b) In the soliloquy inspired by the player's speech (II 2 552) (Page 34).

c) In the nunnery scene (III 1 121) (Page 53).

d) At the end of the play scene where he is exhilarated by his success in catching the conscience in the king (III 2 271). His condition is a contrast here to that of the more phlegmatic Horatio (Page 36).

e) In the bedroom scene where he berates his mother in the most violent language (III 4 41) (Page 42).

f) At Ophelia's graveside where he rants in the most hyperbolic terms (V 1 244) (Page 57).

These moments of excitement, sometimes verging on hysteria, contrast markedly with the apathy and lethargy which dominate Hamlet at other times in the play. It is after the last of these outbursts, at Ophelia's grave, that Gertrude sums up his behaviour:

> This is mere madness,   V 1 278
> And thus awhile the fit will work on him.
> Anon as patient as the female dove
> When that her golden couplets are disclosed
> His silence will sit drooping.

Patrick Cruttwell observes that the modern tendency to play Hamlet as a man who is all the time just a trifle neurotic is out of step with these incidents where, originally, the prince would have behaved in a lunatic manner quite noticeably different from the rest of his behaviour.

There are indications that *Hamlet* reflects a confusion between "madness" and "passion", the meanings of which would in Shakespeare's day be much closer together. Madness is perhaps a more sustained illness than the fits of passion which affect Hamlet. Hamlet's failure to define his own "madness" contrasts with Shakespeare's own definition of the word in the portrayal of Ophelia (Page 57).

MELANCHOLY

Claudius, at one point, describes Hamlet's condition thus:

> . . . there's something in his soul   III 1 167
> O'er which his melancholy sits on brood . . .

52 "Melancholy" is a key word in any evaluation of Hamlet. A contemporary psychological paper, *A Treatise of Melancholie*, by a doctor, Timothy Bright, (later taken up by Burton and expanded into the more famous *Anatomy of Melancholy*) lists the symptoms shown by the "melancholy man", and without doubt some of them apply to Hamlet: "sometimes furious and sometimes merry" – "exact and curious in pondering the very moment of things" – "given to fearful and terrible dreams".

[Elizabethan psychology and medicine were based on the concept of the four humours or bodily moistures: choler, blood, phlegm and melancholia (or black bile). The particular blending of them determined a man's temperament. An excess of black bile produced the melancholy man].

A. C. Bradley* writes:

> One would judge that by temperament Hamlet was inclined to nervous instability, to rapid and perhaps extreme changes of feeling and mood, and that he was disposed to be, for the time, absorbed in the feeling or mood which possessed him. This temperament the Elizabethans would have called melancholic. But this melancholy is something very different from insanity, in anything like the usual meaning of that word. No doubt it might develop into insanity. The longing for death might become an irresistible impulse to self-destruction; the disorder of feeling and will might extend to sense and intellect; delusions might arise; and the man might become, as we say, incapable and irresponsible. But Hamlet's melancholy is some way from this condition and is a totally different thing from the madness he feigns.

Anyone doubting that Hamlet's distemper is distinct from insanity needs only, as we suggested earlier, compare the wild madness of Ophelia and note the contrast (Page 57).

THREE PROBLEMATICAL INCIDENTS CONCERNING MADNESS

There are three incidents in the play which are worthy of notice because it is not clear whether they belong to the realm of Hamlet's assumed madness or his genuine "distraction".

1) THE VISIT TO OPHELIA   II i 74

This is the first reported example of Hamlet's "transformation". Is it a ploy to draw attention to his "antic disposition" and to convince Claudius through Polonius that it has sprung from "neglected love"? Or is it a case of Hamlet's immoderate reaction to his preoccupation with the infidelity of Gertrude and his rejection by Ophelia?

The first point to notice is the disarray of Hamlet's clothes. This is usually taken as the self-neglect of a pining lover, although dishevelled clothing was also part of the pose of the stage madman.

Both Dover Wilson and Wilson Knight remark on the vividness of Ophelia's description:

> Pale as his shirt, his knees knocking each other, II 1 78
> And with a look so piteous in purport
> As if he had been looséd out of hell
> To speak of horrors.

and:

> He raised a sigh so piteous and profound II 1 91
> As it did seem to shatter all his bulk,
> And end his being.

Hamlet would have had to be a supreme actor to create such an effect on Ophelia, perhaps with make-up to represent pallor! They conclude that Hamlet's condition on this occasion is genuine anguish (Page 56).

2) THE "NUNNERY" SCENE   III 1 90

Ophelia has been prevailed upon by Polonius to draw out Hamlet on the subject of their relationship whilst Claudius and he eavesdrop.

The scene begins with Hamlet harping on "honesty" (fidelity) in woman, rather reminiscent of the conversation with Polonius which we considered an example of the "antic disposition" (Page 46). Soon, however, it rises to a vicious attack on Ophelia, which Dr. Johnson called "useless and wanton cruelty", tending to alienate us. What are we to make of it? There seem to be two possibilities:

Either (i) it is a fit arising from Hamlet's disillusionment with women (Page 42) – he says "it hath made me mad".

or (ii) Hamlet is somehow aware of the presence of the king and Polonius and is airing his bitterness that Ophelia should be part of the plot.

There are several theories about Hamlet's awareness of the spies. Harry Levin notices the switch from verse to prose at "Ha, ha! Are you honest?" and suggests that this is the moment when Hamlet spots them. (The director of a production might let one of them be momentarily seen or allow a curtain to move). Another suggestion is that Hamlet's question "Where's your father?" indicates the moment of awareness. Dover Wilson has another idea. He suggests that there is a missing stage direction, "Enter Hamlet unseen" at the moment when Polonius says:

> At such a time I'll loose my daughter to him. II 2 162

This would mean that he was always aware of being spied upon and account for such lines as

> Those that are married already, all but one shall live,

an obvious reference to the listening Claudius.

3) HAMLET'S APOLOGY TO LAERTES

What are we to understand by Hamlet's words to Laertes just before the fencing match? He says:

> . . . you must needs have heard,   V 2 226
> How I am punished with a sore distraction.
> What I have done
> That might your nature, honour and exception
> Roughly awake, I here proclaim was madness.
> Was't Hamlet wronged Laertes? never Hamlet.
> If Hamlet from himself be ta'en away,
> And when he's not himself does wrong Laertes,
> Then Hamlet does it not, Hamlet denies it.
> Who does it then? his madness. If't be so,
> Hamlet is of the faction that is wronged,
> His madness is poor Hamlet's enemy.

This is the longest and most considered speech by Hamlet about his madness. Is it one final example of his clever playing with the device of the "antic disposition", like his words to Rosencrantz and Guildenstern, "my wit's diseased"? (Page 47). Both Johnson and Bradley thought so and blamed Hamlet for taking refuge in a falsehood. Dover Wilson, however, points out that at this stage of the play, it is essential that Shakespeare should ensure our admiration and sympathy for his hero (Page 27). We must, therefore, take it at its face value; a genuine sorrow that Hamlet, in his distraction, has caused such harm.

A Psychologist's Opinion

Whether, in considering the state of Hamlet's mind, we would be nearer the mark by confining ourselves to what the Elizabethans understood by madness, or whether we ought to see his condition as analysable by modern psychological criteria, is a question of approach. However, Hamlet has attracted attention from several 20th century psychoanalysts; Ernest Jones*, one of these, took the case very seriously: perhaps one might find "Hamlet; Denmark, Prince of" in the appropriate place in his card index! He says:

> Shakespeare's extraordinary powers of observation and penetration granted him a degree of insight that it has taken the world three subsequent centuries to reach. Until our generation (and even now in the juristic sphere) a dividing line separated the sane and responsible from the irresponsible insane. It is now becoming more and more widely recognised that much of mankind lives in an intermediate and unhappy state charged with what Dover Wilson well calls "that sense of frustration futility and human inadequacy which is the burden of the whole symphony", and of which Hamlet is the supreme example in literature. This intermediate plight, in the toils of which perhaps the greater part of mankind struggles, is given the name of psychoneurosis, and long ago the genius of Shakespeare depicted it for us with faultless insight.

Chapter 7

Hamlet and Ophelia

Perhaps the greatest puzzle facing the student of *Hamlet* is the relationship between Hamlet and Ophelia. We are never able to get our bearings:

> I did love you once III 1 115

says the prince, and a mere four lines later:

> I loved you not.

What are we to make of these contradictory statements so close together, except possibly that Hamlet himself is not certain of his feelings for Ophelia?

We first meet her giving a spirited reply to Laertes' sanctimonious advice on the subject of Hamlet:

> But good my brother I 3 46
> Do not, as some ungracious pastors do,
> Show me the steep and thorny way to heaven,
> Whiles like a puffed and reckless libertine
> Himself the primrose path of dalliance treads,
> And recks not his own rede.

When Polonius approaches her minutes later on the same topic, she admits that the prince has shown love towards her:

> He hath, my lord, of late made many tenders I 3 99
> Of his affection to me.

but, to her father's request that she see no more of Hamlet, she can raise no spirit, and answers with a subdued and dutiful:

> I shall obey, my lord.

Hamlet's love-letters, later publicised by Polonius, certainly bear out Ophelia's claim that he has importuned her in honourable fashion: we also learn that he has given her tokens of his love. Perhaps, therefore,

Hamlet might have expected more resistance from Ophelia, and perhaps we can understand his thinking that her sudden coldness, following his mother's hasty remarriage, justifies his earlier comment: "frailty, thy name is woman". At any rate, her withdrawal of affection seems to have been too much for Hamlet to bear with equanimity if his reactions in the closet scene, as they are reported by Ophelia, are genuine (Page 52).

In her next meeting with Hamlet she is to be used as bait by the eavesdropping Polonius and Claudius, and her experience is to be a painful "reward" for her dutifulness to her father. She begins by returning Hamlet's love tokens to him, but he denies having given any. Whilst this is literally untrue, perhaps it is circumstantially true in that the Ophelia to whom the prince offered his love is, in his eyes, no longer there; especially if Hamlet knows and remembers that she is at this moment acting out her part in the plot to spy on him, which might also account for his vicious attack on her (Page 53).

[If the time is "out of joint" and "thinking makes it so" (i.e. everything seems unreal and people are not themselves but mutable images in a flickering mind), then Hamlet's apparently contradictory attitude to Ophelia is easily understood. Everything good has changed for Hamlet since his father's time: Gertrude, the court, Rosencrantz and Guildenstern – and Ophelia. The Ophelia of the good days does not exist.]

Whatever her limitations, Ophelia is deeply distressed by Hamlet's words; not for herself but for the change which has come over her erstwhile lover:

> And I of ladies most deject and wretched,   III 1 158
> That sucked the honey of his music vows,
> Now see that noble and most sovereign reason
> Like sweet bells jangled, out of tune and harsh,
> That unmatched form and feature of blown youth,
> Blasted with ecstasy! O, woe is me!
> T'have seen what I have seen, see what I see!

Hamlet and Ophelia next speak together before the play-within-the-play. Here the prince subjects her to comments of cynical and insulting bawdy which some critics have found alienating. A. C. Bradley* writes:

> The disgusting and insulting grossness of his language to her in the play scene . . . is such language as you will find addressed to a woman by no other hero of Shakespeare's, not even in that dreadful scene where Othello accuses Desdemona.

Ophelia's small "sin" of being too acquiescent to her father's wishes (and that may be seen as a fault only perhaps in our 20th century eyes) has brought down upon her inoffensive head all the wrath of Hamlet's morbid and distorted imagination.

But worse is to follow. Ophelia's father is murdered, and this proves too great a burden for her wits. Her madness is obviously intended as a contrast to Hamlet's state of mind. It is so completely rambling and incoherent, a conventional Elizabethan stage madness, that it leads us to wonder whether we could ever see Hamlet's condition as even approaching lunacy. It is a pathetic and lovable portrayal, again opposed to Hamlet's dark and violent cynicism. Some critics have pointed to the ballad of seduction which Ophelia in her distraction sings and have suggested that she is more worldly and less pure than we may have imagined. There can be little doubt, however, that Shakespeare intended us to place Ophelia among the sweet and innocent of this world: he associates her with flowers. There is the gentle pathos of her distribution of various wild flowers to Gertrude and the others, concluding with:

> I would give you some violets, but they withered all,   IV 5 183
> when my father died.

Her suicide is described in terms of flowers and, again an indication of what our attitude towards her ought to be, it is the most beautiful and consciously poetic passage of the play:

> There is a willow grows askant the brook,   IV 7 165
> That shows his hoar leaves in the glassy stream,
> Therewith fantastic garlands did she make
> Of crow-flowers, nettles, daisies, and long purples
> That liberal shepherds give a grosser name,
> But our cold maids do dead men's fingers call them.
> There on the pendent boughs her crownet weeds
> Clamb'ring to hang, an envious sliver broke,
> When down her weedy trophies and herself
> Fell in the weeping brook.

Gertrude scatters flowers on her grave – "sweets to the sweet" – and Laertes pictures violets springing from "her unpolluted flesh". Undoubtedly, she is an innocent victim of the evil in the play.

Hamlet's behaviour during the course of the play can only convince us that, if he did once love Ophelia, all traces have long since disappeared. Yet, when he sees Laertes' gesture of love to her at her graveside, this seems to touch some nerve in him and he becomes violent in his declaration of his love for her:

> I loved Ophelia, forty thousand brothers   V 1 263
> Could not with all their quantity of love
> Make up my sum.

HAMLET AND OPHELIA

How far we can ascribe Hamlet's extravagant conduct here to genuine love of Ophelia, to his unstable mental condition (Page 51) or even to the melodramatic nature of the play, is problematical.

Indeed the word "problematical" sums up the whole nature of the Hamlet/Ophelia relationship. It has been suggested that Shakespeare overstretched himself by taking simple source material (Page 3) and attempting to transform it into something more complex; he found himself short of time and space in the play and was forced to abandon his development of the relationship, thereby leaving it defective. A. J. A. Waldock* wrote:

> We are left with the conclusion that Shakespeare did not trouble or did not wish to make the Hamlet/Ophelia story plainer, and in face of his refusal we are helpless.

Chapter 8

Hamlet and Claudius

A WORTHY OPPONENT

In the traditional revenge play, the hero and the villain would be well-matched and in the outcome of the struggle between them would lie some of the dramatic interest. This element of contest is present in *Hamlet*. The prince, explaining his despatch of Rosencrantz and Guildenstern to England, says:

> 'Tis dangerous when the baser nature comes   V 2 60
> Between the pass and fell incensèd points
> Of mighty opposites.

Hamlet seems almost to relish the cut and thrust of his tussle with Claudius:

> O, 'tis most sweet   III 4 209
> When in one line two crafts directly meet.

He certainly makes little attempt, later in the play, to hide his knowledge of the king's guilt: he taunts him in the play scene and almost invites Claudius to strike at him perhaps because he feels him to be an inferior opponent. This is a dangerous misconception: Claudius is a very worthy adversary and it can be seen, if one follows their relationship, that although Hamlet may get the better of the verbal exchanges, Claudius is always one step ahead in terms of action – until that last unpremeditated and uncharacteristic stroke.

Claudius is a shrewd and efficient politician and a gifted manipulator of other men. As soon as he hears of Hamlet's apparent 'distraction', he is suspicious and his penetrating mind recognizes the truth and spots the danger. Once aware of the danger he soon overcomes the obstacle of Gertrude's love for her son by sending him off to England where he can be killed away from her presence and his death reported back to Denmark as an accident. Hamlet is quick-witted enough to avert this particular thrust, but in informing Claudius by letter of his safety, he makes the mistake of allowing the king time to plan his next move, which might so easily have been successful. The way in which Claudius manoeuvres Laertes is evidence of his cleverness. One moment the irate young man has a sword at the king's throat, the next moment he has been gulled into acting as a cat's-paw for Claudius. Peter Hall writes:

Claudius ranks high in the league of Shakespearian rulers – a superb operator who hardly ever loses his nerve. He is a better actor in the play scene than the players themselves.

And Harley Granville Barker* describes him as

a man who can face the truth, not only about his deed and its deserts, but about himself too. He is in danger, he must act: and it is small wonder that such a weathercock as Hamlet, veering in a spiritual storm, should have, for the time, no chance against him.

A "WHITE" VILLAIN?

We might detect in these two passages a note of respect and admiration, almost of sympathy for Claudius. And yet he is supposed to be the villain of the play! In this lies the problem of Claudius for the producer: he is not entirely a black character. He certainly does not appear to us as villainous as Hamlet would have us believe. His feelings towards Gertrude in the play might best be described as a warm and genuine fondness: he would have disposed summarily of Hamlet but for the queen's love for her son and she in turn

> . . . is so conjunctive to my life and soul,   IV 7 14
> That as the star moves not but in his sphere
> I could not but by her;

although this might be merely a pretext for Laertes' benefit. He does not merit Hamlet's term "satyr". Nor, superficially, does he seem to be "a mildewed ear". On the contrary, his government of Denmark appears strong and stable if we are to judge by the swift and successful settlement of the Fortinbras affair. Set against this stability, however, is his fondness for the "jocund health" accompanied by the gross pomp of the firing of cannon; perhaps more in the spirit of a later Roman emperor than a balanced administrator.

He does not seem to be completely unscrupulous: he shows remorse for his crime:

>   O, 'tis too true,   III 1 49
> How smart a lash that speech doth give my conscience.
> The harlot's cheek, beautied with plast'ring art,
> Is not more ugly to the thing that helps it,
> Than is my deed to my most painted word:
> O heavy burden!

and wishes to be forgiven by God:

> O wretched state! O bosom black as death!   III 3 67
> O liméd soul, that struggling to be free,

Art more engaged; help, angels! Make assay,
Bow stubborn knees, and heart, with strings of steel,
Be soft as sinews of the new-born babe.

Wilson Knight* is Claudius's strongest sympathiser. He praises him for his diplomacy and tact; he sees him as a kindly uncle offering good advice to his troubled nephew; he points to the king's remorse and describes his prayer as "the fine flower of a human soul in anguish". Admittedly, he has less admirable qualities: we must not forget his original crime, his resort to "policy, treachery and skill"; but these faults are forced on him by the action of the play and largely he is characterised by "creative and wise action, a sense of purpose, benevolence" and "love of his queen". He is very human. In contrast to this view of Claudius, Wilson Knight finds Hamlet less than sympathetic. Claudius stands for a positive life force: Hamlet for negative destruction (Page 27).

... OR A "SLIMY BEAST"?

Perhaps Shakespeare intends our attitude towards Claudius to be ambiguous. In life a villain is seldom without redeeming features and evil often appears in attractive clothes. But we must not allow our sympathy for Claudius to obscure the fact that he has committed a "foul and unnatural murder" and that he is the catalyst of evil in the play. L. C. Knights* unequivocally calls him a "slimy beast" and points to the unblushing hypocrisy of his first words in the play:

> Though yet of Hamlet our dear brother's death   I 2 I
> The memory be green, and that it us befitted
> To bear our hearts in grief, and our whole kingdom
> To be contracted in one brow of woe,
> Yet so far hath discretion fought with nature,
> That we with wisest sorrow think on him
> Together with remembrance of ourselves:
> Therefore our sometime sister, now our queen,
> Th'imperial jointress to this warlike state,
> Have we as 'twere with a defeated joy,
> With an auspicious, and a dropping eye,
> With mirth in funeral, and with dirge in marriage,
> In equal scale weighing delight and dole,
> Taken to wife.

And perhaps hypocrisy is the word to explain those passages of remorse in Claudius which we might be inclined to view sympathetically: after all, he is not willing to give up the fruits of his crime but, rather, is prepared to kill again to retain them. Bearing in mind that Claudius is directly responsible for the death of Old Hamlet, Laertes, Gertrude, whom he professed to

62 love, and Hamlet himself, we might find ourselves agreeing with Horatio that the "incestuous, murderous, damned Dane" has been "justly served" with Hamlet's sword.

Chapter 9

The Ghost and others

To some extent it is true to say that the function of every character in *Hamlet* is to provide a contrast to the hero. But this is especially so of three characters: Laertes, Fortinbras and Horatio.

LAERTES

There can be no doubt that we are intended to compare the behaviour of Laertes with that of Hamlet. Hamlet himself points out the comparison:

> I am very sorry, good Horatio, V 2 75
> That to Laertes I forgot myself;
> For by the image of my cause I see
> The portraiture of his.

The two of them are in exactly the same position: but how different is Laertes' reaction! He gathers a crowd in support, breaks through the guards and accosts the king in person, demanding his revenge:

> How came he dead? I'll not be juggled with. IV 5 130
> To hell allegiance, vows to the blackest devil,
> Conscience and grace to the profoundest pit!
> I dare damnation. To this point I stand,
> That both the worlds I give to negligence,
> Let come what comes, only I'll be revenged
> Most throughly for my father.

Surely, he is a model for Hamlet to copy! Yet, if we are inclined to condemn Hamlet, to blame the deaths of Ophelia, Polonius, Gertrude and the others on his delay, we must admit the sad fate of Laertes's prompt action. Because of his impetuosity, he becomes an easy tool for the master politician, Claudius, to use for his own ends. He quickly falls under the king's influence and, in the spirit of the traditional revenge hero, insists on being the organ by which Hamlet meets his death. Without doubt Laertes's motives are, to him, honourable, but they are too naive and ill-considered in the face of this sophisticated evil.

Although Laertes's is a villainous part – to kill the hero – we never see him as a villain: despite the fact that he has inherited something of his father's

64 suspicious, meddlesome nature, if we are to judge from his priggish lecture to Ophelia (I 3), he remains one of the corrupted innocent. He feels sorry for his deed and Hamlet is ready with forgiveness for the noble youth:

> Laertes: Exchange forgiveness with me, noble Hamlet,   V 2 327
> Mine and my father's death come not upon thee,
> Nor thine on me!
> Hamlet: Heaven make thee free of it!

FORTINBRAS

Like Laertes, Fortinbras suggests a parallelism with Hamlet: he too has had a father killed. But also like Laertes, he presents a contrast in character: he is a man of restless energy who must find some field of action to justify his existence:

> Now sir, young Fortinbras,   I 1 95
> Of unimprovéd mettle hot and full,
> Hath in the skirts of Norway here and there
> Sharked up a list of lawless resolutes
> For food and diet to some enterprise
> That hath a stomach in't.

Hamlet again points to the intended comparison by his reaction to the sight of Fortinbras and his army on their way to Poland. Hamlet is stung into another bout of self-recrimination for his lack of action:

> How all occasions do inform against me   IV 4 32
> And spur my dull revenge!

One side of Hamlet's mind wants to regard Fortinbras's enterprise as honourable:

> Rightly to be great   IV 4 53
> Is not to stir without great argument,
> But greatly to find quarrel in a straw
> When honour's at the stake.

Yet Hamlet's feelings in this soliloquy curiously reflect the uncertainty of his response to life (Page 23). He admires Fortinbras and his men:

> This army of such mass and charge,   IV 4 47
> Led by a delicate and tender prince,
> Whose spirit with divine ambition puffed
> Makes mouths at the invisible event,
> Exposing what is mortal and unsure
> To all that fortune, death and danger dare.

But, at the same time, there is an implied criticism that this "spirit of divine ambition" is out of all proportion to the end result, "an egg-shell". It is, on reflection, only doubtfully honourable that twenty thousand men should

> for a fantasy and trick of fame   IV 4 61
> Go to their graves like beds, fight for a plot
> Whereon the numbers cannot try the cause,
> Which is not tomb enough and continent
> To hide the slain.

Fortinbras's main contribution to the play comes at the end, where his timely arrival provides a tidy conclusion to the action. With the evil purged from the state, Fortinbras can promise a future stability which will render the waste of the tragedy worthwhile – "And then a vigorous young lad comes, and says with a charming smile: 'Take away these corpses. Now I shall be your king'". We have already suggested (Page 31) that some directors find this an artificial ending out of keeping with the mood of the play although it cannot be denied that it is appropriate to its overall design – the clouds have been dispersed and the sun will shine again. Perhaps we ought to see in Fortinbras the Hamlet who might have been had he not been tainted by Denmark's corruption.

HORATIO

It is common for a tragic hero to find himself, at some stage in the drama, alone; but no other hero suffers the isolation of Hamlet. The number of soliloquies bears witness to this. Horatio is the only character in the play in whom Hamlet can confide or, indeed, with whom he can communicate.

Compared with Hamlet, Horatio is a simple, straightforward fellow: he is usually content to rubber-stamp the prince's suggestions, and only once does he offer Hamlet advice – good advice – not to accept Laertes' challenge to the fencing match. Hamlet admires him for his integrity and equanimity, most noticeably the latter because this is the quality which Hamlet himself lacks:

> Since my dear soul was mistress of her choice,   III 2 61
> And could of men distinguish her election,
> Sh'hath sealed thee for herself, for thou hast been
> As one in suff'ring all that suffers nothing,
> A man that Fortune's buffets and rewards
> Hast ta'en with equal thanks; and blest are those
> Whose blood and judgement are so well co-medled,
> That they are not a pipe for Fortune's finger
> To sound what stop she please: give me that man

That is not passion's slave, and I will wear him
In my heart's core, ay in my heart of heart,
As I do thee.

Finally, Horatio shows his innate nobility by offering the Roman gesture of suicide with Hamlet (Page 28).

Some critics have noticed a discrepancy in Horatio's character and have accused Shakespeare of slipshod writing. At times he shows himself very knowledgeable about Denmark and its affairs: he is well-informed of the military preparations; Marcellus appeals to him to identify the ghost as that of Old Hamlet and Horatio recognizes it from previous close acquaintance with the king. Yet, on other occasions, he is apparently ignorant of Danish customs and habits (the firing of cannon as Claudius drinks a toast) and has not heard of Yorick or Laertes or Osric. It is as if Shakespeare had two different views of Horatio; perhaps he originally had in mind two separate characters and has failed to reconcile them. Whilst this conflict cannot be denied, we can, however, say that in the theatre it would not be evident; and it would be a mistake to forget that Shakespeare was writing for the theatre and not the study.

THE GHOST

The ghost in *Hamlet* has been called "the most effective of all stage spooks". Certainly, in terms of Elizabethan ghosts the spirit of Old Hamlet is a sophisticated apparition with an unusually long appearance on stage and an inordinate amount to say. Because of this it presents something of a problem for producers. What fails to be awesome can so easily be ridiculous.

Certainly, the spirit is intended by Shakespeare to inspire fear. Marcellus and Bernardo are very jumpy as the play opens: they talk of "this dreaded sight" and Horatio describes how they

distilled   I 2 204
Almost to jelly with the act of fear,
Stand dumb and speak not to him.

Horatio himself admits that

it harrows me with fear and wonder.   I 1 44

Unfortunately, not all productions succeed in emphasising the "hideous" aspect of the ghost as well as that which terrified Partridge in Book 16, Chapter 5 of *Tom Jones* by Henry Fielding. One which didn't is amusingly narrated by Charles Dickens in Chapter 31 of *Great Expectations*.

Ghosts were common devices in Elizabethan theatre for the passing on of information from beyond the grave (Page 6). In fact, quite a conventional lore had been established which indicated what sort of information was likely to be forthcoming, as Horatio suggests at I 1 126.

Shakespeare seems to be intent on establishing the objectivity of this particular ghost; it appears to four different people in the early scenes. Only in the later bedroom scene has it been suggested that the apparition is a figment of Hamlet's overheated brain. However, it was within the power of the ghost to limit its appearance to one person at a time and, having admitted its objectivity in the opening scenes, there seems little point in casting doubt upon it here.

The important aspect of the ghost is its nature.

> Be thou a spirit of health, or goblin damned,   I 4 40
> Bring with thee airs from heaven, or blasts from hell,
> Be thy intents wicked, or charitable . . .

asks Hamlet on first seeing the ghost. It is possible that here is the genuine ghost of Hamlet's father who needs vengeance before his "perturbed spirit" can find rest; but it is equally possible that the ghost is a trick by the devil to tempt Hamlet into unjustified killing of Claudius. Later in the play, Hamlet expresses as much uncertainty on this issue as he did on first confronting the ghost. He claims that he needs proof of Claudius's guilt by means of the play-within-the-play to assure him of the ghost's genuineness (Page 35):

> The spirit that I have seen   II 2 602
> May be a devil, and the devil hath power
> T'assume a pleasing shape, yea, and perhaps
> Out of my weakness and my melancholy,
> As he is very potent with such spirits,
> Abuses me to damn me.

Is this a pretext on the part of Hamlet or a reasonable excuse? This depends on our view of the ghost.

Before the ghost begins its revelation to Hamlet, all four witnesses are understandably dubious. Horatio talks to the "illusion" as one who

> usurp'st this time of night,   I 1 46
> Together with that fair and warlike form
> In which the majesty of buried Denmark
> Did sometimes march.

Hamlet determines to address the figure "though hell itself should gape". He later describes the apparition as having a "questionable shape". Horatio obviously considers it more likely to be an evil spirit when he warns Hamlet:

> What if it tempt you toward the flood, my lord,   I 4 69
> Or to the dreadful summit of the cliff

That beetles o'er his base into the sea,
And there assume some other horrible form,
Which might deprive your sovereignty of reason,
And draw you into madness?

– a significant remark in view of later developments in Hamlet's personality. There is, therefore, plenty of evidence of uncertainty about the ghost at this stage. Later the spirit's message convinces Hamlet that it is "an honest ghost", but perhaps it is only reasonable that with the passing of time the earlier feelings of uncertainty should again make themselves felt.

Chapter 10

The Poetry of *Hamlet*

At the beginning of our survey, we quoted Peter Hall's admonition that it is dangerous to take to pieces an evocative puzzle because we might find ourselves left with the pieces but have lost the magic of the puzzle. Nowhere is this warning more relevant than in our next and very important consideration of *Hamlet*: its poetry; for poetry is delicate to the touch. We appreciate the effect of its presence but when we lay hands on it to analyse that effect, we destroy before we can explain. A. E. Houseman advises us that:

> even when poetry has a meaning, as it usually has, it may be inadvisable to draw it out . . . perfect understanding will sometimes almost extinguish pleasure.

THE EFFECT OF POETRY

The poetry in Shakespeare's plays disturbs the imaginative depths which lie below the physical senses or the rational faculties. It creates in the audience a mood receptive to the ideas of the play; a kind of emotional attuning rather akin to that created by the music behind a film. In fact, that is an apt comparison; for the poetry in poetic drama works unobtrusively, just as good background music does not dominate our consciousness but is nevertheless quietly effective in regulating our mood and warming our responses.

What there is in the poetry to create this effect is difficult to analyse, just as it is difficult to explain why a passage of music affects us in a certain way. Nevertheless, as in music the choice and grouping of notes, the speed of execution, the selection of instrument, repetition, volume, and juxtaposition are contributary factors; so in poetry we have a turn of phrase, a combination of words, a co-ordination of sounds, an evocative image. And if the fusion of these is magically the right one, it will start in us an imaginative reaction, disturbing that which was previously dormant, crystallising that which was previously unformed.

Fortunately for our attempts to understand the poetic achievement of *Hamlet*, we are dealing with a particular kind of poetry – poetry in drama – and in this genre the technical aspects of poetry – rhythm, pace, structure, diction, sound-harmony, imagery – are more amenable to consideration. Poetic drama is a hybrid form where the normal pattern of a poem is married to development of character and movement of plot. In the great

70 Shakespearian tragedies we become conscious of a pervading atmosphere which is generated by these dramatic elements and the poetry working together.

IMAGERY

One means by which this atmosphere is created we have already discussed at some length: the use of the repeated image (Page 16). Not only do these images help us to become aware of the corrupt and hypocritical ambience of *Hamlet*, but they interact with one another acquiring deeper significance with each repetition. The blending of action and imagery gives a coherence and direction to the play.

Lying just outside this sequence of linked images is a wealth of other images which, although not inter-connected, serve to infect our imagination with a sense of dissatisfaction, an encroaching mood of disillusionment:

> Fie on't, ah fie, 'tis an unweeded garden   I 2 135
> That grows to seed, things rank and gross in nature
> Possess it merely . . .

and:

> And duller shouldst thou be than the fat weed   I 5 32
> That rots itself in ease on Lethe wharf,

and:

> So lust, though to a radiant angel linked,   I 5 55
> Will sate itself in a celestial bed
> And prey on garbage

and:

> That one may smile, and smile, and be a villain,   I 5 108

and:

> O God! I could be bounded in a nut-shell, and count   II 2 257
> myself a king of infinite space: were it not that I have
> bad dreams

and:

> God's bodkin, man, much better! use every man after   II 2 533
> his desert, and who shall 'scape whipping?

Hamlet:	Denmark's a prison.	II 2 246
Rosencrantz:	Then is the world one.	
Hamlet:	A goodly one, in which there are many confines, wards and dungeons; Denmark being one o'th'worst	

and:

| In the corrupted currents of this world | III 3 57 |
| Offence's gilded hand may shove by justice. | |

The human spirit, wearied by the emotional and intellectual bleakness of this cynical world, probes beyond to an uncertain metaphysical existence:

| There are more things in heaven and earth, Horatio, | I 5 166 |
| Than are dreamt of in your philosophy | |

and:

what dreams may come	III 1 68
When we have shuffled off this mortal coil	
Must give us pause	

and:

| What should such fellows as I do crawling between | III 1 128 |
| earth and heaven? | |

C. S. Lewis[1] writes of this last extract:

> The real significance of the lines has taken possession of our imagination for ever. "Such fellows as I" does not mean "such fellows as Goethe's Hamlet, or Coleridge's Hamlet, or any Hamlet": it means *men* – creatures shapen in sin and conceived in iniquity – and the vast empty visions of them 'crawling between earth and heaven' is what really counts and really carries the burden of the play.

Perhaps it is meaningful that C. S. Lewis's attempt to explain the poetic effect of Shakespeare's lines is poetic in itself.

The richness of Elizabethan/Jacobean dramatic poetry is drawn from its many-sidedness. So the characters in *Hamlet* cannot be merely emotional and intellectual beings; they must be involved with life at its physical level. This is reflected in the robust glimpses of everyday, earthy existence which punctuate the speculative feelings dominating the play:

[1] C. S. Lewis: *op cit.*

Thrift, thrift, Horatio, the funeral baked meats   I 2 180
Did coldly furnish forth the marriage tables

and:

               a vice of kings,   III 4 98
A cutpurse of the empire and the rule,
That from a shelf the precious diadem stole
And put it in his pocket

and:

Why such impress of shipwrights, whose sore task   I 1 75
Does not divide the Sunday from the week,
What might be toward that this sweaty haste
Doth make the night joint-labourer with the day,
Who is't can inform me?

and:

A little month or ere those shoes were old   I 2 147
With which she followed my poor father's body

and:

For who would bear the whips and scorns of time   III 1 70
Th'oppressor's wrong, the proud man's contumely,
The pangs of disprized love, the law's delay,
The insolence of office,

and:

              this fell sergeant, Death,   V 2 334
Is strict in his arrest.

All these quoted images (which are, despite their number, a small harvest from the play's total yield), affect our sensibility: they are the means by which the poet's thoughts and our thoughts flow together. Keats said that

> poetry should surprise by a fine excess and not by singularity; it should strike the reader as a wording of his own highest thoughts, and appear almost as a remembrance.

This remark touches on the heart of the matter: imagery is absolutely central to poetry because it takes certain aspects of human experience or observation, which at best are only dimly comprehended by the ordinary man, and recreates the experience in words which crystallise our thoughts into an added awareness of whatever is being described. Imagery, by its indirect reference, demands an active and positive response from us which straightforward prosaic, factual statement would deny. Poetry is created for us by our responses – it is the fusion between our personal experience and the poet's expression of his to form a coherent whole within our mind.

DRAMATIC STYLE

Another technical consideration can assist our approach to the expression in poetic drama: the style must be dictated by the needs of the action. We can therefore discuss the style of a passage by reference, for example, to the character who speaks it and the circumstances in which it is spoken.

THE SHAKESPEARIAN LINE. But first a word about the structure of the Shakespearian line. The whole of Shakespeare's verse is based on the use of unrhyming iambic pentameters, known as blank verse. An iamb is a metrical unit comprising an unstressed syllable followed by a stressed syllable (indicated like this: ∪ —). Five iambs in a line constitute a pentameter; so that a perfectly regular line would sound and look as follows:

My lords/we beg/you keep/your seats/awhile.

Obviously a repetition of this steady rhythm throughout a two or three thousand line play would be very monotonous, but comparatively few of the lines in a mature play like *Hamlet* are regular. In fact the strength of the iambic pentameter as the basic component of dramatic verse lies in its flexibility: all sorts of variations (extra syllables, syllables omitted, stressed and unstressed syllables reversed or changed) are possible with the result that innumerable rhythms of natural speech can be reproduced, as our analysis below will indicate. Blank verse makes possible the retention of the credibility of natural speech while creating the effect of poetry.

The scope of Shakespeare's expression is widened when we realise that he can move freely from verse to prose. Any attempts to formulate consistent rules about the situation in which Shakespeare prefers verse to prose (for example, he uses verse for the noble characters and prose for the low characters) are futile in *Hamlet*. The boundary where verse gives way to prose is so blurred as to defy definition. Indeed some areas of verse are in a much lower poetic key than some areas of prose. Again, the discussion which follows will show the indeterminate nature of this border country.

VARIETY OF STYLE. Dr. Johnson praised *Hamlet* for its variety and certainly the enormous range of style in the play would seem to vindicate his opinion. The play opens with a series of short, sharp exchanges designed to reflect the tension and coldness of the situation as the edgy guards fearfully await the anticipated appearance of the ghost:

Barnardo: Who's there?   I 1 1
Francisco: Nay, answer me. Stand and unfold yourself.
Barnardo: Long live the King!
Francisco: Barnardo?
Barnardo: He.
Francisco: You come most carefully upon your hour.
Barnardo: 'Tis now struck twelve, get thee to bed, Francisco.
Francisco: For this relief much thanks, 'tis bitter cold,
            And I am sick at heart.

The same style is used, showing verse at its most flexible, in Hamlet's questioning of Horatio and the others about the ghost:

Hamlet: Armed, say you?   I 2 224
All: Armed, my lord.
Hamlet: From top to toe?
All.   My lord, from head to foot.
Hamlet: Then saw you not his face.
Horatio: O yes, my lord, he wore his beaver up.
Hamlet: What, looked he frowningly?
Horatio: A countenance more in sorrow than in anger.
Hamlet: Pale, or red?
Horatio: Nay, very pale.
Hamlet: And fixed his eyes upon you?
Horatio: Most constantly.
Hamlet: I would I had been there.
Horatio: It would have much amazed you.
Hamlet: Very like, very like, stayed it long?
Horatio: While one with moderate haste might tell a
            hundred.
Marcellus, Barnardo: Longer, longer.
Horatio: Not when I saw't.
Hamlet: His beard was grizzled, no?
Horatio: It was as I have seen it in his life,
            A sable silvered.
Hamlet: I will watch to-night,
            Perchance 'twill walk again.

Again at the beginning of Hamlet's confrontation with his mother the rapidness of the exchange is achieved by speedy movement of the dialogue:

Hamlet: Now, mother, what's the matter?   III 4 8
Queen: Hamlet, thou hast thy father much offended.
Hamlet: Mother, you have my father much offended.
Queen: Come, come, you answer with an idle tongue.
Hamlet: Go, go, you question with a wicked tongue.

```
Queen:   Why, how now, Hamlet?
Hamlet:  What's the matter now?
Queen:   Have you forgot me?
Hamlet:  No, by the rood not so,
         You are the queen, your husband's brother's wife,
         And would it were not so, you are my mother.
Queen:   Nay then, I'll set those to you that can speak.
```

A marked contrast to this almost naturalistic conversational verse is to be found in Claudius's speech explaining why he has married Gertrude. The occasion is hypocritically formal and the expression is correspondingly high-flown, imitating, as it does, the artificial and affected style which we call euphuistic. The term is taken from John Lyly's book 'Euphues' (1580), a treasure house of florid courtly utterance. The style is characterised by complex sentences, elegant balances and cadences so elaborately contrived as to preclude sincerity; all of which elements are strongly present in the first sixteen lines of Claudius's speech:

```
King:  Though yet of Hamlet our dear brother's death        I 2 I
       The memory be green, and that it us befitted
       To bear our hearts in grief, and our whole kingdom
       To be contracted in one brow of woe,
       Yet so far hath discretion fought with nature,
       That we with wisest sorrow think on him
       Together with remembrance of ourselves:
       Therefore our sometime sister, now our queen,
       Th'imperial jointress to this warlike state,
       Have we as 'twere with a defeated joy,
       With an auspicious, and a dropping eye,
       With mirth in funeral, and with dirge in marriage,
       In equal scale weighing delight and dole,
       Taken to wife: nor have we herein barred
       Your better wisdoms, which have freely gone
       With this affair along – for all, our thanks.
```

It is worth noting that the entire extract consists of only one sentence and that the main verb and whole point of that sentence does not appear until line fourteen, being held at a distance by "though . . . and . . . that . . . and . . . yet . . . that . . . therefore", with the result that the important piece of information – "taken to wife" – appears so much a cadence that it might almost (intentionally?) escape notice. An aesthetic fascination with the graceful balances of the three lines preceding "taken to wife" might also cause the courtiers' ears to slide over this alarming news.

In this situation Claudius uses the stylistic device as a pleasing mask to cover the ugly face of adultery and regicide. Later he employs the same style to divert the anger of Laertes. Notice the convolutions and devolutions of:

> That we would do IV 7 117
> We should do when we would: for this 'would' changes,
> And hath abatements and delays as many
> As there are tongues, are hands, are accidents,
> And then this 'should' is like a spendthrift sigh,
> That hurts by easing;

all designed to sooth Laertes before springing upon him the swift challenge:

> but to the quick o'th'ulcer – IV 7 122
> Hamlet comes back, what would you undertake
> To show yourself your father's son in deed
> More than in words?

The surprise attack is a success and Laertes becomes Claudius's tool:

> To cut his throat i'the church.

On both of these occasions there is a purpose in employing euphuistic expression, but Shakespeare does not always use it seriously. In *Henry IV Part I* he gloriously satirizes the style when Falstaff, acting the part of the king, makes his marvellous mock-heroic speech to his "son", prince Hal, in the tavern at Eastcheap:

> Harry, I do not only marvel where thou spendest thy time, but also how thou art accompanied: for though the camomile, the more it is trodden on the faster it grows, yet youth, the more it is wasted the sooner it wears. That thou art my son, I have partly thy mother's word, partly my own opinion; but chiefly, a villainous trick of thine eye and a foolish hanging of thy nether lip, that doth warrant me. If then thou be son to me, here lies the point; why, being son to me, art thou so pointed at? Shall the blessed sun of heaven prove a micher and eat blackberries? a question not to be asked. There is a thing, Harry, which thou hast often heard of, and it is known to many in our land by the name of pitch: this pitch, as ancient writers do report, doth defile, so doth the company thou keepest; for, Harry, now I do not speak to thee in drink, but in tears, not in pleasure but in passion, not in words only, but in woes also.

There is probably a similarly satirical element in Rosencrantz's sycophantic speech to Claudius, complete with epic simile:

> The single and peculiar life is bound   III 3 11
> With all the strength and armour of the mind
> To keep itself from noyance, but much more
> That spirit upon whose weal depends and rests
> The lives of many. The cess of majesty
> Dies not alone; but like a gulf doth draw
> What's near it with it. O, 'tis a massy wheel
> Fixed on the summit of the highest mount,
> To whose huge spokes ten thousand lesser things
> Are mortised and adjoined, which when it falls,
> Each small annexment, petty consequence,
> Attends the boist'rous ruin. Never alone
> Did the king sigh, but with a general groan.

On the whole, the use of this style is suggestively appropriate to the insincere and smarmy superficiality of the Danish court and significantly it falls to Polonius to take it to the extremes of parody:

> Polonius: My liege and madam, to expostulate   II 2 86
>   What majesty should be, what duty is,
>   Why day is day, night night, and time is time,
>   Were nothing but to waste night, day and time.
>   Therefore since brevity is the soul of wit,
>   And tediousness the limbs and outward flourishes,
>   I will be brief – your noble son is mad:
>   Mad call I it, for to define true madness,
>   What is't but to be nothing else but mad?
>   But let that go.
> Queen: More matter, with less art.
> Polonius: Madam, I swear I use no art at all.
>   That he is mad 'tis true, 'tis true, 'tis pity,
>   And pity 'tis 'tis true – a foolish figure,
>   But farewell it, for I will use no art.
>   Mad let us grant him then, and now remains
>   That we find out the cause of this effect,
>   Or rather say, the cause of this defect,
>   For this effect defective comes by cause:
>   Thus it remains, and the remainder thus.

A more wholesome use of measured phrasing is to be found in Hamlet's speech to Horatio immediately preceding the play within-the-play:

Since my dear soul was mistress of her choice,   III 2 61
And could of men distinguish her election,
Sh'hath sealed thee for herself, for thou hast been
As one in suffering all that suffers nothing,
A man that Fortune's buffets and rewards
Hast ta'en with equal thanks; and blest are those
Whose blood and judgement are so well co-medled,
That they are not a pipe for Fortune's finger
To sound what stop she please: give me that man
That is not passion's slave, and I will wear him
In my heart's core, ay in my heart of heart,
As I do thee.

This well-turned compliment shows Hamlet at his most relaxed and gentlemanly, but the mood is interrupted – "Something too much of this" – by the imminent arrival of Claudius and his courtiers so that the remainder of the passage is, by contrast, business-like, efficient and direct in its movement:-

        Something too much of this –   III 2 72
There is a play to night before the king,
One scene of it comes near the circumstance
Which I have told thee of my father's death.
I prithee when thou seest that act afoot,
Even with the very comment of thy soul
Observe my uncle – if his occult guilt
Do not itself unkennel in one speech,
It is a damnéd ghost that we have seen,
And my imaginations are as foul
As Vulcan's stithy; give him heedful note,
For I mine eyes will rivet to his face,
And after we will both our judgements join
In censure of his seeming.

A similar contrast, but in reverse, is to be noted in the "nunnery" scene where the rising emotional urgency of Hamlet's prose:

I have heard of your paintings too, well enough.   III 1 145
God hath given you one face and you make yourselves
another, you jig, you amble, and you lisp, you nick-
name God's creatures, and make your wantonness your
ignorance; go to, I'll no more on't, it hath made me
mad. I say we will have no mo marriage – those that
are married already, all but one, shall live, the rest
shall keep as they are: to a nunnery, go,

gives way to Ophelia's formal verse-portrait of the changed Hamlet:

> O, what a noble mind is here o'erthrown! III 1 153
> The courtier's, soldier's, scholar's, eye, tongue, sword,
> Th'expectancy and rose of the fair state,
> The glass of fashion, and the mould of form,
> Th'observed of all observers, quite quite down,
> And I of ladies most deject and wretched,
> That sucked the honey of his music vows,
> Now see that noble and most sovereign reason
> Like sweet bells jangled, out of tune and harsh,
> That unmatched form and feature of blown youth,
> Blasted with ecstasy! O, woe is me!
> T'have seen what I have seen, see what I see!

Contrast is used on another occasion: the rhetorical style which Hamlet employs to describe the ideal renaissance man, an important concept in the play:

> What a piece of work is a man, how noble in reason, II 2 307
> how infinite in faculties, in form and moving, how
> express and admirable in action, how like an angel
> in apprehension, how like a god: the beauty of the
> world; the paragon of animals; and yet to me, what is
> this quintessence of dust?

(Page 50) is given emphasis by being placed just before the more prosaic discussion on contemporary theatre.

Another passage, this time at the end of the same discussion, also stands out by contrast: Hamlet's introduction to the player's speech, which is distinguished by its hyperbolic, bombastic expression, reminding us of *Hamlet's* melodramatic antecedents, the revenge plays:

> 'The rugged Pyrrhus, he whose sable arms, II 2 456
> Black as his purpose, did the night resemble
> When he lay couchéd in th'ominous horse,
> Hath now this dread and black complexion smeared
> With heraldy more dismal: head to foot
> Now is he total gules, horridly tricked
> With blood of fathers, mothers, daughters, sons,
> Baked and impasted with the parching streets,
> That lend a tyrannous and a damnéd light
> To their lord's murder. Roasted in wrath and fire,
> And thus o'er-sizéd with coagulate gore,

With eyes like carbuncles, the hellish Pyrrhus
Old grandsire Priam seeks' . . .

The exaggeration of both style and content of this passage is approached
in *Hamlet* proper on only one occasion: when Hamlet fights with Laertes in
Ophelia's grave:

'Swounds, show me what thou't do: V 1 268
Woo't weep? woo't fight? woo't fast? woo't tear thyself?
Woo't drink up eisel? eat a crocodile?
I'll do't. Dost thou come here to whine?
To outface me with leaping in her grave?
Be buried quick with her, and so will I.
And if thou prate of mountains, let them throw
Millions of acres on us, till our ground,
Singeing his pate against the burning zone,
Make Ossa like a wart! nay, an thou'lt mouth,
I'll rant as well as thou.

Here we see Hamlet apparently at his least calm, but the physical behaviour
prior to this speech is so uncharacteristic of him that one wonders whether
or not the prince is acting (theatrically) in the way the revenge convention
would expect of him.

On the other hand, one can point to moments earlier in the play when
the style of Hamlet's speeches reflects what is certainly a genuine torment
in his mind:

That it should come to this,   I 2 137
But two months dead, nay not so much, not two,
So excellent a king, that was to this
Hyperion to a satyr, so loving to my mother,
That he might not beteem the winds of heaven
Visit her face too roughly – heaven and earth
Must I remember? why, she would hang on him
As if increase of appetite had grown
By what it fed on, and yet within a month,
Let me not think on't . . . frailty thy name is woman!
A little month or ere those shoes were old
With which she followed my poor father's body
Like Niobe all tears, why she, even she –
O God, a beast that wants discourse of reason
Would have mourned longer – married with my uncle,
My father's brother, but no more like my father
Than I to Hercules, within a month,
Ere yet the salt of most unrighteous tears

Had left the flushing in her galléd eyes
She married.

The disjointed construction of the lines is appropriate to the jerky and disconnected thoughts expressed; as if the concepts swirling in Hamlet's mind are too reprehensible to be admitted. Fragmented rhythms are similarly used to convey Hamlet's agitation as his consciousness, fighting to comprehend the significance of the ghost's revelation, jumps incoherently from one idea to another:

> O all you host of heaven! O earth! what else?   I 5 92
> And shall Í couple hell? O fie! Hold, hold, my heart,
> And you, my sinews, grow not instant old,
> But bear me stiffly up . . . Remember thee?
> Ay thou poor ghost whiles memory holds a seat
> In this distracted globe. Remember thee?
> Yea, from the table of my memory
> I'll wipe away all trivial fond records,
> All saws of books, all forms, all pressures past
> That youth and observation copied there,
> And thy commandment all alone shall live
> Within the book and volume of my brain,
> Unmixed with baser matter – yes by heaven!
> O most pernicious woman!
> O villain, villain, smiling, damnéd villain,
> My tables, meet it is I set it down
> That one may smile, and smile, and be a villain,
> At least I am sure it may be so in Denmark . . .

The breathless and uneven movement of those lines, designed to reproduce a mind on the verge of being overwhelmed, is opposed in style to other moments when Hamlet is at his most philosophical. There is a restrained and meditative proportion and a careful, logical graduation in the "To be or not to be" soliloquy; the balancing of possibilities in "To sleep, perchance to dream", the remorseless catalogue of "natural shocks" presented in the form of rhetorical questions.

The passionate and the contemplative Hamlet is distinguished by style as well as content.

'UN-POETRY'. We have dealt at some length with the practical side of style because this workman-like use of language adds to the substance of the play and demonstrates Shakespeare's technical skill. Ultimately, however, it is not the practicability of the verse which leaves an impression on us, but the imaginative effect of the poetry.

Life is full of mystery which sometimes our minds can grasp but seldom retain. Poetry illuminates that mystery. L. C. Knights suggests that Hamlet's personality defies analysis because "it is revealed through the poetry." He is "the expectancy and rose of the fair state", a "dull and muddy-mettled rascal"; a man who wishes that the "Everlasting" had not "fix'd his canon 'gainst self-slaughter"; one who claims to realise the "special Providence in the fall of a sparrow"; a man who has "bad dreams" but "a noble heart".

If we cannot succeed completely in analysing the contribution that poetry makes to *Hamlet*, we can perhaps indicate its measure in a negative way. We can ask ourselves what would happen to our response if the poetry were not there. C. S. Lewis[2] writes:

> If, instead of the speeches he actually utters about the firmament and man (in II, 2), Hamlet had merely said "I don't seem to enjoy things the way I used to", and talked in that fashion throughout, should we find him interesting? I think the answer is "Not very".

Similarly, if, instead of

> what dreams may come
> When we have shuffled off this mortal coil
> Must give us pause,

he had contented himself with a banal statement like "I wonder what it's like to be dead", or instead of:

> I could be bounded in a nutshell and count myself a
> king of infinite space; were it not that I have bad
> dreams,

he had merely said, "I'd feel better if I weren't so depressed", we would be considerably less impressed.

The poetry enhances the basic situation, giving it a vaster significance and creating in us a deeper response, a feeling that in *Hamlet*, "the real and lasting mystery of our human situation has been greatly depicted".

[2] *ibid.*

Chapter 11 ✗

Hamlet in Production[1]

We suggested earlier (Page 1) that when our microscopic armchair scrutiny was complete we ought to see a production of *Hamlet* so that the relevance of the minute particles to the play's total design would become clear. After all, Shakespeare did write his plays to be performed; a truism which our more erudite literary critics have occasionally been guilty of forgetting. Consequently, some of the ideas formulated in the study may be considerably less valuable if they are found to be unworkable in practice. This is not to say that the work of the scholar has no bearing at all on the staging of *Hamlet*: the theatrical fashion and the language of Shakespeare are nearly four hundred years old and, because of this, need interpreting – the province of the scholar – with the result that a director who works out a Shakespearian production without reading some of the appropriate literary criticism may well find his offering unacceptably off-course. And, whilst a director has many factors to consider, some of them very mundane – the physical and vocal qualities of his available actors, the restrictions of the stage, the use of costume and lighting and music, the nature of scenery and props, even the timing of the intervals – his point of embarkation must be the question of interpretation. Which ideas in the play does he wish to stress? Which items to soft-pedal or even ignore? The scholar can help him to solve these initial problems.

In the study of Shakespeare too little importance has been attached to the work of directors. A production has somehow been thought of as a fleeting phenomenon, as ephemeral as the hastily-conceived first-night press notices which, a year later, often constitute its only available record. But if we allow that a good director's interpretation achieves for hundreds of people in the multiple dimensions of the theatre what a literary critic does for one person at a time in very limited scope, then we might feel able to benefit from a more leisurely and more permanent consideration of significant productions. To this end, as a bookish substitute for an actual performance of the play, we shall round off our introduction to *Hamlet* by recalling some presentations. We shall ask ourselves the questions: what in the play seemed important to the director? What steps did he take

---

[1] Quotations in this chapter are taken from directors' personal notes, programme notes, and interviews recorded by the author. Other quotations, from various first-night press reviews, are indicated (**R**).

to ensure that his ideas were conveyed to the audience? How far did the audience understand and accept the director's interpretation?

But which production shall we choose? Here again the problem of *Hamlet's* popularity threatens to overwhelm us since even to list the memorable presentations would cause a gross imbalance in our current approach. Richard Burbage, David Garrick, John Philip Kemble, Edmund Kean, William Charles MacReady, Henry Irving, Johnston Forbes-Robertson, Herbert Beerbohm Tree, Sarah Bernhardt: the names of the great actors (and actress!) who have played the Prince of Denmark read like the chapter headings of a *National Biography of Players, 1600–1900*. In our own century there have been well over a hundred major productions of *Hamlet* in London and Stratford alone and, once more, the actors' names are as familiar in the mouth as household words: John Barrymore, John Gielgud, Lawrence Olivier, Alec Guinness, Paul Schofield, Michael Redgrave, Richard Burton, Peter O'Toole. It was with some justification that at the turn of the century Max Beerbohm lamented: "In England *Hamlet* has long since ceased to be treated as a play. It has become simply a hoop through which every eminent actor must, sooner or later, jump".

The story of *Hamlet* productions is the history of drama. Every change in theatrical fashion can be marked by a *Hamlet* milestone. Should we look at the nineteenth century extravagances of Beerbohm Tree, which concentrated on minute correctness of period and costume, sometimes cutting as much as a third of the Shakespearian text to allow more room for spectacle? Should we consider the attempts of William Poel and Harley Granville-Barker to reproduce a livelier *Hamlet* closer to the original Elizabethan spirit? Or the landmark of Barry Jackson's production in 1925 which, because it was done in modern dress, allowed a fresh wind to blow away the dust of tradition with the result that the actors, feeling a new freedom, made the problems of the prince and the Danish court immediate to the contemporary audience? Or the bowdlerised versions? Or the productions which swept away the cluttering paraphernalia of ornate sets?

One thing is certain: we cannot attempt them all. We shall therefore take the line that since, inescapably, we are moderns, the *Hamlets* most interesting to us will be modern ones; and, accordingly, using the criterion of contemporary relevance rather than immortality or greatness, we shall consider two productions:

a) Peter Hall directing David Warner at Stratford in 1965.

b) Trevor Nunn directing Alan Howard, also at Stratford, in 1970.

Peter Hall directs David Warner

If Peter Hall was right to say that '*Hamlet* is a mirror which gives back the reflection of the age which is contemplating it' (Page 3), then it follows that by slanting the play's direction its contemporary relevance can be highlighted:

There are many subjects in *Hamlet*. There is politics, force opposed to morality; there is discussion of the divergence between theory and practice, on the ultimate purpose of life; there is the tragedy of love as well as family drama; political, eschatological and metaphysical problems are considered. There is everything you want, including deep psychological analysis, a bloody story, a duel, and general slaughter. One can select at will. But one must know what one selects and why.

The writer of this passage, Jan Kott*, saw a production of the play in Cracow in 1956 in which the director had selected a *Hamlet* which portrayed in terrifying clarity the uncertainty of life in a satellite country of the Eastern Bloc. Everyone in the play was constantly being watched; marriage, love and friendship, everything was corroded by fear. The play became a drama of political crime in a state where politics had destroyed all natural feelings and affection. Kott admits that what he saw was a simplified *Hamlet* but one with startling relevance to Poland of the mid-20th century.

Ten or so years later (first in 1965, revived in 1966) another *Hamlet* was presented in Stratford, in which Peter Hall as director set out to show the social relevance of the play to contemporary western civilization. He started from the premise that there ought to be an immediate empathetic connection between us and *Hamlet* because it was written in a time of doubt when "the boundless vigour of the Renaissance was failing, and the glorious Elizabethan age was, like its monarch, in decline. Shakespeare himself was entering a dark valley – a place of tragedy, cynicism and disgust.' Correspondingly few people would deny that our own age seems to have lost not only the creative energy which nurtured our society but the sense of purpose which gave it direction:

> It is natural that the play is most completely revealed to times of doubt: to Shakespeare's own, to the Romantics, and, I think, to ours. In times of settled beliefs, such as the 18th century, its complexity could be suspect and its enigmas indulgent. It abounds in great questions and refuses to give answers.

DISILLUSIONMENT AND APATHY. Hall suggested that the problems facing the future of the Western world are so daunting that we seem to lack the will even to begin to tackle them and are therefore suffering a universal malaise of apathy stemming from disillusionment:

> For a man said to do nothing, Hamlet does a great deal. He is always on the brink of action, but something inside him, this disease of disillusionment, stops the final, committed action.
>
> In particular it is the young who feel out of touch with the community into which they are growing, and they evince uneasiness at their inability to effect change. Faced with what they consider the monolithic hypocrisy and false values of their elders in positions of power, they find their idealism stifled. The consequent disillusionment is an emotion which you can encounter in the young today. To me it is extraordinary that in the last 15 years the young of the West, and particularly the intellectuals, have by and large lost the ordinary, predictable radical impulses which the young in all generations have had. . . . This negative response is deep and appalling.

86   This "negative response," which was to be the touchstone to Hall's production of *Hamlet* found expression in the direction of David Warner's
prince, who was to be a young (Warner was twenty-three) student figure

> trembling on the point of full maturity . . . He has within him the possibility
> of all virtues or all vices, but at this crucial point in his development he is
> tried by an extreme crisis,

and the crisis was to be seen as the sudden crumbling away of all the beliefs
which had sustained his growing-up:

> He is crucified by an experience so complex that it leads to a profound dis-
> illusionment and finally to a terrible fatalism.

Hall's youthful – radical – social – existential – political direction (if we
might paraphrase Polonius) provoked a rather nervous and, as usual,
divided response. But, willy-nilly the critics, here was Hall's offering and
it undoubtedly appealed to younger theatre-goers as

> a *Hamlet* comprehensible to our age, and the proof of the Hall-Warner pudding
> could be heard in cheers from the young on the first night. It can also be seen
> from the queues of young people clamouring to see the play, for this *Hamlet*
> is immediately recognisable as a child of our time. (R)

Perhaps a production which fired the young might by definition be
anathema to the (older?) critics! Yes, agreed one (younger?) reviewer:
"as soon as young Prince Hamlet stops being predictably beautiful, like
Bach, and starts sounding like Bartok there is trouble. Once Hamlet the
Dane ceases to 'glitter' – a word synonymous with a middle-class conception
of a honey-tongued monarchy – then people start sounding off about verse
being butchered, liberty-taking with Shakespeare and similar claptrap."
If this indeed were the reason for the largely unfavourable reception of
Hall's interpretation, it might ironically vindicate his view of Hamlet as a
young man disillusioned by the corrupt and fettered standards of his
elders, an example of an Elizabethan generation gap.

Nevertheless there is a distinct danger that an idiosyncratic interpretation
might neglect aspects of the play which cannot textually be ignored:

> The only trouble with [Hall's] theory (that a disillusioned Hamlet should be
> characterised by disinterested apathy) is that Hamlet cannot possibly escape
> involvement because the ghost of his dead father is constantly provoking
> him on to vengeance. If his father hadn't been murdered and his mother
> hadn't married the murderer, the play wouldn't exist. To symbolise these
> highly personal events as something from which Hamlet can escape – like a
> university student who doesn't want to think about the bomb – is a distortion
> that can only result in confusion and muddle. (R)

Can there really be a disinterested Hamlet ("To be or not to be – he's not
bothered") in a play so obviously concerned with passion? It was generally
felt that in his keenness to realise his vision Hall had virtually ignored important factors: "the theme of Hamlet's revenge and Hamlet's delay – the

essential content of the play, I am orthodox enough to think – is evidently an embarrassment to the director", resulting in "a bizarre and perverse portrait . . . only peripherally linked to the Hamlet of Shakespeare".

On the other hand, some critics were happy to accept Hall's direction as an intelligent and moving experience which was "better in intellect and emotion than any conventional interpretation one is likely to see for some time".

Because of the peculiar nature of this play, any production must rise or fall by the portrayal of Hamlet and, generally speaking, David Warner's playing was adversely criticized with the blame being apportioned between Warner's delivery and Hall's direction of the role. It was, however, the appearance of the prince as a modern undergraduate which attracted the most immediate attention, and the tone adopted was sometimes quite scornful:

> We are offered Hamlet as a coward, a boy who doesn't know what has hit him, who is prodded into action only when he cannot escape it (to save his own skin). He is a Hamlet who knows he will never kill Claudius as he knows he should. He is a Hamlet with a 'Ban the Bomb' button. (R)

and:

> David Warner is a sketch for a college swot, raggedy red muffler hanging around his neck, steel spectacles, and an impression of having outgrown his black corduroy suit. Princes may look how they like, of course, but this picture of one of nature's uncaring outsiders conflicts irritatingly with his hyper-sensitivity. It is a quibble, but seems to typify the lack of coherence in the character. (R)

Yet behind this perhaps rather glib debunking there was the widely-held feeling that Hall had had to pay too high a price for his emphasis of Hamlet's disillusioned apathy. Other important ingredients in the character were lacking: warmth, stature, urgency, pride – "This Hamlet has no pride. He is a snuffy little post-graduate student from Wittenberg who is pitch-forked into a situation he cannot even begin to cope with".

One reviewer wished that

> this tiresome, perverse and self-indulgent creature could be got out of the way (like Rosencrantz and Guildenstern). Something has gone seriously wrong with a production that so alienates sympathy from the hero. (R)

One is forced into asking the question whether, if there is such alienation, there can be tragedy.

ISOLATION. We might well offer our sympathy to a lonely man, and Warner's Hamlet was certainly alone. Even Horatio, his traditional confidant, almost vanished so as to preserve his isolation. Having no one to turn to, Hamlet was forced to ask the audience for help, and this he did through the soliloquies, which he delivered directly from the front of the stage to the up-turned faces in the auditorium, thus establishing

> an intense rapport which is rarely obtained by more fluent and sonorous Hamlets. (R)

It was felt that this unconventional use of the soliloquies was a successful coup, "probably the greatest triumph of the production":

> Using the Elizabethan convention with total literalness, Hamlet communes not with himself, but with us. For the first time in my experience, the rhetoric, spoken as it was intended to be, comes brilliantly to life. (R)

Of course, not everyone was happy: one reviewer felt that Hamlet's clashes with Gertrude, Claudius and Ophelia were robbed of any emotion and impact because of the cold and clinical manner in which the soliloquies were delivered as "donnish lectures rather than private searchings of a man's own soul."

INADEQUACY. Hall's treatment of the Ghost was thought to be revealing:

> the key to every Hamlet is its ghost. A solid ghost demands an active, believing hero, thwarted by events; an insubstantial one, all light-effects and echoes, a brainsick prince, nerveless and Oedipal. (R)

Many directors are embarrassed by this most "skittish" of Shakespearian spirits and try to hide it behind the battlements, but Hall's version was a giant construction: an impressive ghost, unless you chose to describe it as "a ten foot tall puppet rolling soundlessly about in the shadows like a Dalek" or to remember that Horatio had recalled the ghost's appearance in minute detail "without ever apparently feeling it necessary to add that the old boy had doubled his height in the underworld." This overwhelming figure was made to "dwarf his shuddering child in a dark commanding embrace," thereby conveying Hamlet's dependence on his father in a strik-ing tableau which was, suggested one critic, to indicate Hamlet's real problem, a feeling of inadequacy in the face of his father's stature (the less usual side of the Oedipus coin):

> Every recollection of his mission is a reminder of his sonship, his immaturity. His pretence of madness is half an admission of this. He shelters in childishness, seeking to appear not merely too insane to be responsible for his actions, but too young. His disguise is not just dishevelment but the wilful untidiness of an undergraduate, the half-baked impertinence of the adolescent who would test his parents' love to the limit of tolerance . . . The easiest disguise for an adolescent with a problem too big for him is that of a problem adolescent. (R)

Hamlet does not avenge because he is not yet adequate to do so.

CLAUDIUS, OPHELIA AND GERTRUDE. If this were the case, it would follow logically that, in an effort to avoid the issue of revenge, Peter Hall's Hamlet would divert his thoughts elsewhere. Thus he occupies his attention by being disillusioned, firstly with the hypocrisy of the Danish court and secondly by sex. Claudius is the figure-head of evil in Denmark. On stage he appears as

> a tough, steely and ruthless manipulator, . . . a fascinating figure, plainly a master of the power game. He uses all his skill, first to win over Hamlet, then to destroy him.

There was an electric moment at the end of the play scene when he and the prince stood calmly face to face and he silently accepted that the play had been a challenge to a fatal duel. The only weakness noted in this portrayal of the King was that he seemed untouched by guilt and the lines which convey guilt were spoken awkwardly. Hall wanted Hamlet to see right through Claudius and Polonius (a shrewd right-hand man with none of the conventional doddery foolishness): Hamlet was to understand that 'as politicians they have to lie and cheat' but he was to be unable to accept this fact of life.

Hamlet's disillusionment with the sexual mores of Denmark is, in Peter Hall's opinion, more grounded in the text than imagined:

> To the ghost, as to him, the murder takes second place throughout the play to the enormity of adultery. This obsession leads Hamlet to question what marriage is, and finally to the refusal of Ophelia. Like many men in crisis, he takes it out on the weaker person.

Unfortunately for this point of view, the Ophelia of the production could not readily be construed a weakling. She was a novel Ophelia but one could not imagine why she should go mad or kill herself; she was a

> quacking deb, shrill in her aggressions, dangerous in her anger . . . a Chelsea-set beatnik who could swap obscenities with Hamlet any night. She seems more likely to smoke pot than go potty at her father's death. (R)

The obsession with Gertrude's adultery was brought out very strongly in the closet scene, perhaps to the point where exaggeration touches absurdity; it became:

> a sick game played for kicks as he rolls ruttishly on top of her, pleading to hear the lascivious details of her love-making. (R)

Perhaps the best aspect of Hall's direction of Gertude was that he solved the problem of her age – old enough to be Hamlet's mother but young enough to provoke the King's lechery – by giving her a youthful wig which she removed (like Queen Elizabeth I) at bedtime to reveal her true age.

CONCLUSION. Hall differed from Trevor Nunn (Page 99) in that he did not intend an optimistic resolution for Hamlet. Far from emerging, on his return from England, to a calm, almost cheerful acceptance of the nature of things, he was finally to arrive at a "terrible fatalism".

The experience of living dirties, warps, and makes us suffer. The play finally says that revenge is wrong, yet Hamlet is wrong not to revenge. Would he be right to revenge? What would happen? We know from the other plays that he would suffer, he would die, blood would have blood. But *Hamlet* does not say in any simple way that death is the great leveller, that what is tragic is man's mortality: but rather, that we need to discover and understand the universe in anguish, possibly, certainly more cruelly and realistically than the philosophers. And in this reality, which Hamlet comes to, lies the greatest suffering of all.

I don't find *Hamlet* a tragedy in the sense that at the end of it I am left ennobled, purged, and regenerated. I think it belongs with *Troilus and Cressida* and *Measure for Measure* as a clinical dissection of life. It is a shattering play, a worrying play: and at the end you are left with Fortinbras, the perfect military ruler. And I don't know about you, but I would not particularly like to live in Denmark under Fortinbras.

This aspect of the production seems to have been most clearly conveyed and best appreciated. The final scenes saw the player Hamlet and the production *Hamlet* coalesce and achieve a high tension. The duel scene was played quietly and Hamlet "with a polished fatalism, meets death as a black joke which has at last rid him of the whole nauseating mess".

> When Mr Warner's Hamlet comes to the speech about there being a special providence in the fall of a sparrow, he cannot bring himself to believe that that providence extends also to him. There are no wings in which he can trust. He goes to his death unreconciled, unabsolved, but also unabsolving . . . He says the readiness is all, and for an instant his face quivers. He makes great efforts at mastering himself and then, condemned but not now afraid, walks off the stage firmly. (R)

He died with a burst of laughter which might be interpreted as "an existentialist's discovery that the universe is absurd and history a trap". The overwhelming impression was one of loss. This failure of Hamlet to solve the problems of his disillusionment in a positive way was nicely summed up:

> Warner gives us a Hamlet tuned totally to the modern key – the young intellectual poised on the brink of maturity . . . He looks to God and finds no sense or compassion there; to the example of his elders, which has worn paper-thin; to the strength of politics, which he finds corrupt; to love, which has soured; to the act of sex, which is degraded, and to his fellow men, whom he finds full of the same folly inherent in man from first breath to last. In the end he clutches at death as a great belly-laugh – from nothing to nothing, between which is nothing.

On the whole, the response to Hall's production was one of disappointment and unacceptance although there were those who appreciated that he had been striving for a new and worthwhile interpretation and had gone some way to achieving it.

DELIVERY. Outside the debate on interpretation, there were also doubts about the momentum of the production (although allowances were made for first night lack of polish). There were references to its "funereal pace"; it killed all the excitement inherent in the action. Hall used a very full text but it was presented at "a very slow pace which gives the emotion contained in the words a chance to seep away and lose itself". David Warner's "dictation-speed delivery" was criticized because it entailed "a sacrifice of tempo, some magic of the poetry and much dramatic impact."

This mention of the word poetry introduces another batch of criticism. It was felt that in searching to reveal new meaning appropriate to the production David Warner (with a voice which could "fray into monotony") was guilty of mangling Shakespeare's verse. The production paid too little attention to "metrical accuracy and coherence":

> A realistic and dramatically effective moment is often given too great precedence. If the lines –
>
>   Soft you now,   III i 88
>   The fair Ophelia – Nymph, in thy orisons
>   Be all my sins remembered –
>
> are spoken for their own metrical, rhythmic and tonal qualities in contrast with those of the preceding lines, they must surely be spoken softly, flowingly, with a concluding long phrase. Indeed any actor who chooses to interpret 'Nymph' and 'orisons' satirically, will find that the run of front vowels makes them hard words to stress, to punch or bite; and he will have to fight against syntax and metre to escape a growing ease – almost a relaxation – in the concluding words. David Warner, however, takes violent grasp of the speech so that his Hamlet addressed Ophelia with growing volume and power and with a whirling movement away.
>
> Another example of momentary disregard of the implicit stage-directions of Shakespeare's versification is found in the same scene with Ophelia's compact and ordered soliloquy; here Glenda Jackson [Hall's Ophelia] breaks rhetorical and metrical regularity by shouting out loud, as if to the spying king and father, the words "The observ'd of all observers", so the break which Shakespeare has provided in the following "quite, quite down" is lost, and calculation rather than hard-won control and sentiment becomes dominant.[2]

But, mangling apart, there was a feeling that Warner spoke his part dully and without poetry, which may have been deliberate. One reviewer, whilst not approving of this unpoetic rendering, thought the tone of the language fitting for the tone of the whole production:

> It is, on its deliberately small scale, a very intelligent lost-soul Hamlet. He thinks his way into every line, and we are obliged to go with him, though I kept on wondering whether it could be a translation into prose, an answer to an examiner's demand for a paraphrase. Young playgoers, I am sure, have no complaint about this. Many of them are listening to *Hamlet* for the first time; and here is an actor able to explain to them lucidly what he is thinking, and to remain at the same time the kind of fellow they might reasonably meet, any afternoon. It is a most painstaking Hamlet diagram; and it does not seem to matter that excitement is sacrificed, that any splendours of sound are muted, and that theatrical glory has turned to a rather scruffy realism.

---

[2] J. Russell Brown: 'The Royal Shakespeare Company in 1965' in *Shakespeare Survey* 19.

I can listen with respect to Mr Warner as he expounds the meaning of the soliloquies. When he says 'I do not know why yet I live to say "This thing's to do"', I realise that it is a key to his performance, and that I ought not simply to remember how magnificently Olivier spoke the same phrase in 1937 (Agate's description was "trumpet moaned"). Yet, all said, some of us do need more than determined exposition and a recognisable gaucherie, engaging at times, at others not. We are determined enough to ask for a larger excitement, for a sense of language; we ask to be genuinely moved, and I doubt whether the 1965–model Hamlet will stir this in some of his more experienced listeners. (R)

Trevor Nunn directs Alan Howard

On the one hand:

> It is a little sad to go to a festival in Shakespeare's birthplace to his greatest play and come away so unsatisfied. (R)

but on the other hand:

> Anyone who can faithfully pursue the character of Hamlet through a four-hour performance has my undying admiration for stamina. Anyone who can give a fresh and credible idea of the character, as Alan Howard did last night, has my undying admiration for intelligence. (R)

These divergent opinions of Trevor Nunn's 1970 production exemplify the objections of those who work in the theatre that they do not get a fair deal from the reviewers: the critics are mere "showtasters" who "judge a play by a single sampling, in the artificially fraught conditions of a first night" who "decide its future in three tense unnatural hours as brutally and superficially as the 11-plus decides a child's".

To remedy this unsatisfactory state of affairs, Ronald Bryden for *The Observer* spent some time (but not enough, he admitted) with the company during its six weeks of preparations. He heard Nunn's initial talk outlining his intentions and watched progress for six days of the fourth week of rehearsals. After this experience he concluded that he would never again be able to see a first night as a thing in itself, to be judged in isolation; he had become involved in the fears and hopes of the production; he had discovered the actors' real work, the growing into their parts, as he tells us about Alan Howard's Hamlet:

> When I joined the fourth week of rehearsals, he was playing Hamlet as a glittering, sardonic concealer of his genuine feelings, the most adept Machiavellian in a Machiavellian court. As a verbal swordsman, the Renaissance avenger chuckling over death's jest-book, he was impressive but glacial—I thought, gloomily, that this would be a Hamlet definitive in a kind I had no wish to see.
> But there were still gaps in his characterisation, holes he walked round or through, muttering or throwing away the lines while significant hush fell over the rehearsal hall. They were the lines where Hamlet is not acting: the soliloquies, 'Give me the man who is not passion's slave', 'The readiness is all'. Tactfully, the other actors waited for him to show his hand, pressing him only where their own playing required answering violence to spark from.

But it was clear that his performance must be the tent-pole, to whose height, and no higher, the production would rise.

Gradually, as I watched, he mastered his reticence. Slowly elaboration fell away; the sardonic camouflages and dazzling escape devices. His performance grew more and more still and, as it did so, amazingly younger. It was as if he was stripping from himself not only years, but the defensive armour, the competence to hide the child in the adult, which they had brought. The jeering glances, the sharp small-toothed smiles diminished. In their place emerged a dark, smouldering stare of misery, a sudden, dismayed fall of the mouth, like a child who has been slapped.

Bryden felt that he had profited considerably from his more systematic watching: he was able to weigh Nunn's total design against his stated intentions, and found it brilliant.

In his prefatory talk to the actors, Trevor Nunn seemed to envisage three thematic strands weaving through his intrepretation:

1) There was to be a fluctuation between faith and doubt. Hamlet had grown up in an orthodox Catholic environment but had attended Wittenberg University, a hot-bed of Lutheran questioning of orthodoxy. Which, if either, was right?

2) The key scene was to be the play scene as the production set out to explore the disparity between thought and will, word and action, facade and inner reality. Nunn said:

> The tragedy is riddled with theatrical language, with various uses of the "play-the-part" idiom, and with words like "act", "perform", "prologue", "shape", "applaud", and "show" which are either overtly theatrical, or else hover on the edge of a dramatic meaning. The play of the "Murder of Gonzago" is not only the strategic centre of the plot, the turning-point of the action; it is also . . . the focal point from which a preoccupation with appearance and reality, truth and falsehood, expressed in theatrical terms, radiates both backward and forward in time . . . Through the agency of illusion, the prince has at last separated appearance from reality, hypocrisy from truth. The theatre has been his touchstone.

3) Following particularly from this adoption of the players, the theatre and acting a part as the central figuration of *Hamlet*, there was to be an examination of the shift between feigned madness (the 'antic disposition', the player's whole function suiting with forms to his conceit) and real madness:

> If we pose, how long will it be before the pose becomes our real self? If we wear a mask, how long before our face grows to fit it? If Hamlet pretends to be mad, how long before the reality overtakes him?

Nunn began his talk by admitting that the interpretation of a play is a highly subjective matter – hence directors – and the interpretation of *Hamlet* is more subjective than most.

> Every cut is an act of interpretation discriminating between one approach and another. There is no perfect *Hamlet* – as Hamlet says, the purpose of playing is to show each age its form and pressure.

So what was this Hamlet to be about?

I once saw a graffito on a wall, which said:
There was a young man who said Damn,
It appears to me that I am
Allowed only to move
In a predestined groove;
Not a bus, not a bus, but a tram.

Is the individual, then, in control of his own destiny? – Compare the effects of 'the complete Renaissance man' with, say, the great plague. If you are a Catholic, you answer a resounding "yes": salvation comes through good works. But one day a man called Luther banged up ninety-nine objections to the Catholic Church – on a door in Wittenberg. This is where Hamlet, a prince from a great warlike but religious (religiose?) background, went to university; leaving behind doting parents, school friends like Rosencrantz and Guildenstern, a gawky kid called Ophelia, the acclaim and popularity of the entire Danish population; and taking with him all the training and grooming that a future king must have.

Alan Howard managed to convey successfully the impression that he had once been "the expectancy and rose of the fair state". The implication was that Hamlet's university surroundings would seriously disturb his youthful complacency, but:

whatever shock Wittenberg was to his previous beliefs and criteria, it could have been nothing to the shock of being told one day that his father, who only recently had won a famous victory in single combat, was dead.

The set and the costumes were designed to convey Scandinavian coldness, an aspect of the production which received universal praise. It was a wholly Scandinavian court:

hinting of Northern barbarity with its white furs and cold silver jewellery (R)

and, for once:

these Danes, wrapped and befurred in glacially white sheepskins, look like inhabitants of some rigorous northern clime (R)

When Hamlet arrived in Elsinore, he was faced with two other shocks:

his uncle had been elected king, and this same uncle was spending all his time with Hamlet's mother. After a brief period of mourning, they announce that they are to be married. They marry, official mourning is ended, celebrations begin, centred on the happy couple; and Hamlet is told that under no circumstances may he return to his friends at university. All this happens to a young man who believed that human beings are close to angels (What a piece of work is a man'), that he is part of a divine plan and death does not happen without reason. These events, and what happens immediately after, must make him challenge everything he has believed, persuade him that man is a beast, that life and death are irrational, without plan or purpose, that God may not exist and individual action of any kind is futile and worthless.

THE COURT SCENE. Nunn's production made a very strong point of Hamlet's appearance in I 2; he was outstanding in black against everyone's white, designed to give the impression of a wedding celebration. This was the first inner-council meeting; not exactly business but a time when they could celebrate with the newly weds, who in their turn, could acknowledge general goodwill:

> And, therefore, for Hamlet to turn up dressed for a funeral is no mere individual indulgence but actually a gross public statement of shattering impact. There is a formal dress for this occasion to mark the end of official mourning – and somebody turns up and deliberately keeps it going. A terrible silence falls upon the place: it is the person who has entered wearing a sports jacket and drunk at a big formal function and the first thing that everyone does is to take it in and the second thing is to assume that he is not there, otherwise the entire proceedings will be disrupted, which is why Hamlet is left to the last. There is a defiant going on with the celebrations as if he does not exist and then an attempt by Claudius to deal with him quietly – 'What are you doing? Listen to your mother, listen to me' – and we get the impression that it is Hamlet who insists on making it public. It is not Claudius who is trying to manipulate and assert his power over Hamlet; Hamlet is making the first move by turning up in such a way.

After this, another shock for Hamlet's already turbulent mind:

> A Ghost, claiming to be Hamlet's father, claiming to have come from a Catholic-sounding purgatory, accuses his brother Claudius of murder and incest.

(Trevor Nunn's direction of the Ghost is a good example of how many ideas may have to be amended in practice, so that good effects at rehearsal are lost in production. Originally the dead king was to be a real and palpable "apparition", as Horatio describes him, and in rehearsal the actors had developed a natural fear of his close proximity. Unfortunately, when the scene was transferred into the theatre proper, it was discovered that the unseasoned wooden floor creaked and the effect so carefully nurtured was immediately destroyed. It was necessary to switch to a static and more distant ghost, which was never as satisfying.)

"TO BE OR NOT TO BE". The ghost risks eternal damnation for his son by demanding of him one action, revenge: "At that moment Hamlet's problem becomes specific." The revenge commission acted as a sort of catalyst which pricked Hamlet on to think about other more fundamental questions, and the resultant inner-debate was often bitter and savage, as for example, in the "To be or not to be" soliloquy. Nunn had this set in a chapel with Hamlet kneeling in a pew. The chapel was to be used for important scenes later and was a symbol of the ordered faith which had been shattered in Hamlet and which he was struggling to regain. It was also a place which could be defiled and desecrated by the current regime as it was on this occasion by Polonius and Claudius who used confessionals as bases for spying. In these circumstances the soliloquy had a ring of cynicism:

"To sleep perchance to dream; ay, there's the rub" was not an acceptance of the situation as an unlockable Gordian mystery but actually a bitter accusation: That's the catch you seem to have organised for us, Catch 22 – it was very savage. Consequently the whole series of examples of the whips and scorns of time was not reflective but actually a kind of challenge, it was saying "Big deal! What a wonderful world has been designed for us to endure! What does it consist of? It consists of every kind of abuse with no way out, no simple solution!" So that "Their currents turn awry" was a conclusion for Hamlet: he admitted, "I can't get beyond it; I'm defeated by the thought of either being the cause of someone else's death or of ending my own life. I don't know what to believe – in the faith my mother taught me or what I've been learning recently? Can I believe in the Ghost? I'm trying to sort it out but I can't even be sure whether man is sublime or ridiculous, an angel or a beast. What is the position? Until I know all this, how can I act?"

THE "ANTIC DISPOSITION".

Hamlet has been the observed of all observers; now he must be the observer of all observed. How can he be detached, outside, so that he can assess? He finds a near-perfect solution: the feigning of madness, which gives him the liberty to see other people as they really are and allows him to say and do whatever he likes – he thinks. But the things that have happened to him have left their marks; will he always be able to know when madness is feigned; is the feigning of madness a subconscious rationalisation of his real condition? Is Polonius entirely wrong in thinking that Hamlet's madness is caused by unrequited love? Since Hamlet has returned, he has found only one person to declare himself to and at the precise moment when he needs Ophelia most, she is commanded to have nothing further to do with him. As far as Hamlet is concerned, Ophelia is as fickle as his mother. Are Claudius and Gertrude entirely wrong in detecting in Hamlet signs of dangerous lunacy? Are we in fact only to believe Hamlet about Hamlet?

THE PLAYERS. As Trevor Nunn continued the questioning which was to be the basis of his production, he reached the point where the theme of real and pretended madness dovetailed with the theme of theatrical and actual performance.

Does the actor always know the impact of his performance? Does he know when the performance has become more real to him than life? Two months elapse between the moment when Hamlet first conceives the idea of performing madness and the moment when we first see the performance. It is a long time for the distinction between art and life to stay unblurred – if indeed the distinction was ever clear to him in the first place. Just as we suspect that the performance is comfortable for him, is in itself a solution to the problems of life, a group of travelling players arrives at Elsinore. For these players performing is their livelihood. In all senses, without performing they could not exist.

The metaphor that life is a play ('All the world's a stage and all the men and women merely players') is a commonplace but, as Trevor Nunn saw it, in *Hamlet* the image reverberates through the whole substance of the play. As Hamlet witnesses the first player's speech, he is shocked and forced to reassess the reality not only of his own actions but also those of everyone else around him: who is real, who merely playing a part?

First, Hamlet sees and experiences a grief more real in the player over Hecuba than he is capable of for his own dead father. But the player is performing and Hamlet is real. Second, in his violent temper in the "rogue and peasant slave" soliloquy he is amazed to discover that he himself is performing. Third, he sees that Claudius is also performing (the role of innocence) and hits on the idea – which had proleptically occurred to him much earlier with the words "He that plays the king shall be welcome", that a performance of recent events may involve Claudius to the extent of dropping his own performance and revealing the reality – "the play's the thing wherein I'll catch the conscience of the king".

The play will be necessary because:

> the ghost may be a performer: all the evil that Hamlet sees may be illusion, for there is nothing either good or bad but thinking makes it so.

There are so many other performances too: Ophelia performs a part to Hamlet with Claudius and Polonius as audience; Hamlet, already lost in his performance of madness, thinks he is capable of getting a fellowship in a cry of players; Polonius was an actor at the university where he played Caesar and, significantly, was killed by Brutus; Gertrude is set to perform a catechism to her erring son with Polonius as audience; Laertes rants and mouths in his sister's grave. Only Horatio, it seems, does not perform, until he tries to play the antique Roman.

To distinguish the theatrical players from all these other players, Trevor Nunn had them perform the play-within-the-play in a highly stylised manner like something out of the Japanese Kabuki Theatre, and in brilliant colours as opposed to the uniform black and off-white of the Danish court; and the performance was to be the watershed of the action:

> The players bring down, or at least accelerate, disaster but, more important, they "suit the action to the word, the word to the action". It is this union of word and action that is very close to the centre of *Hamlet*. . . . in life there is a continual disparity between word and deed. . . .
> From the very first [Hamlet] has claimed to be united in word and deed: he knows not "seems"; not for him "The actions that a man might play".

By contrast he has become aware of disparity in others. What did his mother really think as she followed his father's body to the grave? How could she be so apparently grief-stricken and yet say 'yes' to Claudius? How could Ophelia, who said one thing, suddenly act differently? Rosencrantz and Guildenstern speak of friendship but are engaged in spying on him. We can imagine, then, the astonishment in Hamlet when he perceives the same disparity in himself – he can fall a-cursing, but can do nothing. . .

> Hamlet cannot show himself his father's son in deeds more than in words, because no action will fit his words. Action is too crude for the prince who considers too curiously and who quarters thoughts. "Words, words, words" says Hamlet. He is fascinated and infatuated by language and he is incredibly and dextrously articulate. Mad or sane, perplexed or clear, words never fail him, but no action will suit.

If, however, the players can solve the problem of suiting the action to the word, this could be Hamlet's way to resolution too. After the departure of the players, Hamlet was made to dress in a monk's robe and cowl which one of the players had discarded. In this 'costume' he spoke the soliloquy, "'Tis now the very witching time of night", in a deliberately melodramatic way as if he were hamming the part of the exulting revenge villain. This element of performance had been in evidence at the beginning of the play scene when Hamlet had spoken his lines to Ophelia like a comic, but as the scene ended the distinction between reality and acting became increasingly obscure. Hamlet's donning of the monk's black habit caused him to choose and assume a role, that of confessor, and just as he was working himself into his part, ready to confront his mother, Claudius blurred reality and performance still further by coming forward and kneeling for his supposed soliloquy on the very spot where the players had enacted the murder. Hamlet consciously "acted" his part in the ensuing prayer scene.

It was in the closet scene, however, that the two strands of performance and madness really become entwined as Hamlet was made to enter the reality of madness through the medium of his performance. Playing the confessor to his terrified mother's penitence, he was so carried away by his performance that it became real to him. On discovering Polonius, instead of the usual casual stab through the arras, Hamlet performed what began as a calculated act of ritualistic theatre but finished as a brutal and frenzied butchery, with the old man being stabbed repeatedly and eventually collapsing and dragging down with him the curtain behind which he had been hiding. Something had snapped in Hamlet's brain so that the consciously invoked mood of the soliloquy which had closed the play scene had passed from playing to reality. Yet Hamlet, still carried along by the power of his performance, failed to understand the actuality of his deed. His deliberate scene-ending couplet,

> This counsellor
> Is now most still, most secret and most grave,
> Who was in life a foolish, prating knave

was spoken with a flourish and it would not have seemed out of place for Hamlet to bow to the audience. (It followed from all this that when Hamlet apologised to Laertes immediately before the duel, he was speaking what he considered to be the truth; that when he killed Polonius, he had been mad.)

Still in his acting mood, still wearing his monk's habit, Hamlet played the clown to Rosencrantz and Guildenstern's questions, eventually escaping to hide among a crowd of real monks in the chapel. For a time there was confusion and consternation as the guards tried to pick out Hamlet from the others. When he was found and brought before his uncle, Claudius ripped off the habit to reveal Hamlet almost naked, whereupon Claudius lost control and savagely punched him several times in the stomach, a desecration of the religious surroundings. The beatings brought Hamlet back to reality for the first time since the beginning of the play scene.

When Hamlet next appeared, on his way to England, he had been physically forced into line and this was shown by his being dressed in the white furred clothes which the audience had come to associate with the Danish court:

> For the first time he appears as a member of that obscene establishment and therefore he is unrecognisable to begin with; we really do not know who it is who is asking the captain questions. He has become a functionary, compelled to toe the line but at the same time we can also see that, as far as he is concerned, just to be able to get away from that place is a temporary solution – the pressure has been somehow removed. He is already thinking clearly, his role playing finished; one must try to get over the sense of really lucid and cogent debate in the soliloquy beginning "How all occasions do inform against me". His metaphysical preoccupations about "What is a man" are still there, but now he is totally in control; he is talking retrospectively about the beast, the monster which had overwhelmed his mind, and clearly his reason is restored. He is a man who has been very ill, who is recovering. The trip to England is a sort of convalescence.

CONCLUSION. All around Hamlet, people have been acting; and now that Hamlet himself has been a player, what has he learned from his performance? As he faces death in the final moments of the play, what answers does he have to the questions which have plagued him: what is life, what is death; what is good, what is bad; what is heaven, what is hell; what is man, what is God?

> When everything is over, we can look back with Horatio on recollections of
> carnal, bloody and unnatural acts,
> Of accidental judgements, casual slaughters,
> Of deaths put on by cunning and forced cause
> And, in this upshot, purposes mistook
> Fall'n on the' inventors' heads.
> No special providence then in the fall of a sparrow; no divinity shaping our ends; no divine plan: just a squalid, nasty mess. All action has been futile. Hamlet only acts after he has been condemned to die, and when action can give him no satisfaction.

Almost casually, therefore, did Alan Howard dispose of Claudius, who, for his part, drank the poison almost willingly as if this were the conclusion demanded by the script of a play.

> For Hamlet, drawn to his death, all problems fade. There is only one tragic reality to be faced – about eternity only seconds away; and that is summed up by Hamlet in the short phrase, "the rest is silence".

Alan Howard could conceive this no other way but the final conception of sudden horror; not:

> there is nothing else worth talking about

but:

from this moment, there is nothing there,

a split-second perception of sempiternal nothingness.

Many of the first-night press reviews accepted the intelligence of Trevor Nunn's *Hamlet*, although they were less certain whether he had succeeded in conveying his vision. As it happened, Nunn would have agreed with them since he himself remained unsatisfied: something had been lost in transferring his ideas to the stage. Some critics, however, felt that there were grounds for questioning the validity of the interpretation. 'When it comes to the crunch', said one, 'Shakespeare's Hamlet is not mad; Alan Howard's is.' Another suggested that the production was off-course because it directed sympathy away from a trouble-making Hamlet and towards a long-suffering Claudius. Trevor Nunn admitted that this might be the case, but did not accept that it necessarily invalidated his view of the play.

> I think that the balance of the play is such that if we are fundamentally unsympathetic to Hamlet's predicament and personality, then we really can't follow the play through to its conclusion. But it is a great mistake to assume that the opposite is true: that, unless we are constantly in sympathy with Hamlet and never deviate from total sympathy with his position, the play won't work; because it seems to me that our sympathy is strained on so many occasions. I think, for instance, that we have a period of time when we understand Laertes and go along with him.

OPHELIA. The "nunnery scene" too is a point where Hamlet is likely to lose sympathy because of his violent behaviour towards Ophelia. Trevor Nunn accepted this danger but defended Hamlet's right to a share of consideration and compassion. He has declared himself to Ophelia as the only person in whom he could confide his emotions, when suddenly the contact is broken:

> He is incredibly upset by that. At the end of "To be or not to be", when Hamlet becomes aware of Ophelia kneeling in a nearby pew in the chapel, his 'Nymph, in thy orisons' is ironic but with strong suggestion of the love that has existed between them and has been betrayed. Ophelia is overwhelmed by the situation and tries to communicate something of her real feelings whilst having to stick to the text demanded by her listening father. Hamlet, however, can only see an Ophelia who is negating a true and real relationship by returning his tokens in a totally unconvincing way; she is playing a part. The realisation of this (without any revelation of the hidden audience) causes something to snap in Hamlet and he becomes violent and unstoppably savage, because he has been deceived.

The same savage mockery carries through to the "country matters" exchange, a public degradation for Ophelia; and it is not until the funeral that Hamlet can reveal his true feelings for her:

> He actually picks her up; it is very macabre, but absolutely unmistakable, inescapable that this is the truth – "I loved Ophelia" – and that's what a great deal of it has been about; that's where so much of it has gone wrong.

Hamlet 1965: Peter Hall directing. *"Our chiefest courtier, cousin, and our son."*

"Are you honest?"

*Claudius appears to find
Gertrude desirable.*

Hamlet with the gravedigger.

Hamlet 1970: Trevor Nunn directing.

Hamlet gives advice to the players.

Claudius interrogates Hamlet about the disappearance of Polonius.

*The mad Ophelia in black
contrasts markedly with the
white of the court.*

Preparations for the duel scene.

Section 2
Discussion

The Character of Hamlet

1.

.According to Aristotle's survey of the nature of Greek tragedy in *The Poetics*, the main purpose of tragedy is to arouse in the audience a feeling of pity for the hero and a sense of terror[1]. Pity is easily enough defined as sympathy with the plight of the hero. Terror is more difficult to define in modern terms: in the original Greek the word really means a kind of healthy respect for the powers of the gods, a warning to man not to conceive too high an opinion of himself. (Greek tragedies were of a religious nature). There is a connection with the Christian phrase "fear of the Lord"; a feeling of 'there-but-for-the-grace-of-God-go-I'.

Any failure on the part of the dramatist to gain sympathy for the hero and identification with his condition tends to detract from the purity and poignancy of the tragedy.

Most people can identify themselves sympathetically with Hamlet, but Charles Marowitz is vulgarly outspoken in his condemnation of Shakespeare's most famous tragic hero. He says:

> I despise Hamlet. He is a slob, a talker, an analyzer, a rationalizer. Like the parlour liberal or the paralysed intellectual, he can describe every facet of a problem, yet never pull his finger out.

Obviously for him, Shakespeare has failed.

Examine your attitude towards Hamlet as the play progresses and say whether you find yourself at all in agreement with Marowitz's opinion.

2.

Hamlet has been described as "melancholic, introspective, . . . incomprehensible and gracious." Could you defend this choice of adjectives?

3.

Many critics find Hamlet a changed man on his return from the sea-voyage. Can you detect any change in his attitudes? Does he seem perhaps less agitated? less bitter and cynical? less subject to frustrating doubt and self-analysis?

[1] See Appendix I page 130.

the experience + crude
knowledge —symbols.

4.

Hamlet's madness is one of the problems of the play which have attracted a lot of controversial attention. Sometimes Hamlet seems to claim for himself freedom from any taint of madness whatsoever:

> It is not madness III 4 141
> That I have uttered; bring me to the test,
> And I the matter will re-word, which madness
> Would gambol from.

At other times he says that he is merely 'mad in craft':

> I am but mad north-north-west; II 2 382

On one occasion he says:

> I'll no more on't, it hath made me mad. III 1 149

To determine the nature of Hamlet's state of mind, divide into three groups: one to seek out those passages of the play which seem to support the idea that Hamlet really is distracted; one to find those where feigned madness is indicated; one to examine those incidents which are perhaps a fusion of the two conditions.

You might like to consider the following points:

a) how we in the 20th century view madness.

b) what the Elizabethans thought of madness. *King Lear* offers a very full study of contemporary attitudes in its presentation of no less than three madmen: the fool, a professional "madman"; Edgar, who adopts the disguise of poor mad Tom; and Lear, who is driven mad by the cruelties of his daughters. Webster's *The White Devil* would also prove a valuable contrast since there are indications that Cornelia in that play, maddened by the death of her son, is based on Ophelia, and Flamineo's assumed melancholy owes something to Hamlet. In Webster's *The Duchess of Malfi* we see a "mad-scene" designed to be funny.

c) how the concept of Hamlet's madness has been filtered from the earlier versions of the story.

d) what Hamlet himself says about his madness; what he does; how the other characters diagnose the prince's state of mind and whether their comments can be accepted at their face value.

e) how Hamlet's condition can be contrasted with that of Ophelia in IV 5.

5.

In the early versions of the Hamlet story, the hero feigned madness in order to divert suspicion whilst he proceeded with his revenge. Examine Act I Scene 5 and consider why Hamlet assumes an "antic disposition". If the reason is to divert suspicion, does he succeed? Is there perhaps a feeling that as the play progresses Hamlet, far from taking steps to remain secretive, actually invites a confrontation with Claudius?

6.

Several critics have stated their opinion that Hamlet cannot easily bring himself to perpetrate his promised revenge because he cannot be sure that revenge, although traditionally accepted, is morally justifiable. As late as V 2 he appears to be seeking assurance from Horatio that he would be right to kill Claudius:

> . . . is't not perfect conscience
> To quit him with this arm?

They see Hamlet as a figure of doubt in an age of doubt. Examine what Hamlet says about his desire to kill Claudius and his delay in doing so, and say whether you feel there is any evidence either in the text or in the atmosphere of the play to lead you to accept the view that Hamlet's inaction is due to a moral scruple about the ethics of revenge.

7.

Some critics have maintained that Hamlet does not delay in perpetrating his revenge, but in fact kills Claudius as soon as circumstances permit. Can you defend this view? Notice Hamlet's vehement promises to the ghost to exact immediate vengeance in I 5; consider his conviction of the ghost's genuineness – "It is an honest ghost" – and compare this with his motives for staging the play-within-the-play. Consider his behaviour in the prayer scene, especially in the light of Claudius's last words in that scene, and Hamlet's words as he kills Polonius only a few minutes later. Contrast the directness with which Laertes accosts the king.

8.

When Hamlet examines his reason for delay in the three soliloquies beginning:

O, what a rogue and peasant slave am I	II 2 553
To be or not to be	III 1 56

(This soliloquy is ostensibly about suicide but it would seem that in the closing lines Hamlet's inaction is subconsciously troubling him) and:

How all occasions do inform against me	IV 4 32

he diagnoses some form of cowardice. Consider what Hamlet does during the course of the play and make out a case to refute the self-accusation of simple cowardice.

Look more carefully at what Hamlet means by cowardice in the soliloquies. Does this weaken the case you have just propounded?

9.

The passage in I 4 23-38

> So oft it chances in particular men . . .
> . . . To his own scandal

is thought to be defective; hence its obscurity of meaning. Yet it is an important passage because it is usually taken as an oblique reference to the tragic fault or excess which causes the downfall of the tragic hero. Rephrase the passage in your own words so as to give it meaning.

Often enough in Shakespeare's tragedies, the hero's fault is clear enough. Othello is gullible and jealous, and these two weaknesses in his character make it possible for Iago to manipulate him to murder the innocent Desdemona. Macbeth is ambitious and too susceptible to the influence of his more single-minded wife. Lear is vain, old and lacking in judgement and self-knowledge. Antony is disposed to gratify his sensuality rather than follow the dictates of his reason.

Discuss the nature of Hamlet's tragic fault[2].

10.

In III 1, Hamlet says to Ophelia:

> I did love you once.

Four lines later he says:

> I loved you not.

Bearing in mind the circumstances in which these two lines occur, divide yourselves into two groups, one to gather evidence in order to advocate the view that Hamlet loves Ophelia, the other to oppose that view. You might like to consider the following incidents: Ophelia's conversation with her brother and father in I 3; her account of Hamlet's visit to her closet in II 1; Hamlet's love letters broadcast by Polonius in II 2, together with the old man's opinion that Hamlet's distraction is a direct consequence of Ophelia's rejecting him; Hamlet's treatment of Ophelia in III 1 and during the play-within-the-play in III 2; and Hamlet's behaviour at Ophelia's grave in V 1.

[2]See Appendix 1 page 130.

Hamlet might like to think of himself as witty.

To the Elizabethans wit meant, firstly, good judgment and discretion, and secondly, a quickness of intellect and a liveliness of invention manifested as a capacity for apt expression and a talent for saying brilliant and sparkling things. Falstaff sees himself as the epitome of this second concept of wit when he says of himself in Act I Scene 2 of *Henry IV Part 2:*

> I am not only witty in myself, but the cause that wit
> is in other men.

Examine the places in the play where Hamlet employs his wit and consider what light it throws upon his character or state of mind.

You might like to consider the following: Hamlet's conversation to Rosencrantz and Guildenstern in II 2; the "To be or not to be" soliloquy in III 1; and Hamlet's speculations in the graveyard scene, V 1.

12.

"O, what a noble mind is here o'erthrown!" says Ophelia. Would the nobility of Hamlet's mind have been evident without Ophelia's comment?

Other Characters

1.

Laertes has a specific function in *Hamlet*; he is to act as a foil to Hamlet, he is to represent the traditional revenge hero with whom Hamlet can be compared. He is Hamlet's opponent, yet we feel sympathy for him. Consider why you do feel this sympathy towards Laertes. (You can always argue against this viewpoint, but it is worth noting that Hamlet praises Laertes). Does it detract from Hamlet's stature as tragic hero for us to feel this way towards his opponent and would-be murderer?

Points you might like to consider are Laertes' rather priggish advice to Ophelia in I 3; his prompt action in demanding satisfaction from Claudius for the death of Polonius in IV 5; the king's manipulation of Laertes as his cat's-paw in IV 7; the two confrontations with Hamlet, at the graveside in V 1 and during the fencing match in V 2, together with the reconciliation between them, also in V 2.

2.

In common with other tragedies of the time, *Hamlet* presents a number of deaths. When a character dies, we are given a final opportunity to appraise our feelings towards him, and those feelings will often be a reflection of how we thought of him while he was alive. Perhaps you feel antipathy towards a character but somewhere in your mind is a corner of pity. Perhaps you are torn between admiring or despising a character. Perhaps you think that a character has been insufficiently developed to arouse any reaction in you.

In this light, analyse your feelings towards Gertrude, Ophelia, and Rosencrantz and Guildenstern.

3.

It is usual to portray Rosencrantz and Guildenstern as two sycophantic fops. Some producers, however, see them as quite efficient and dangerous spies who are outwitted by an opponent cleverer than they are. Which viewpoint would you adopt? Is it possible to look on Rosencrantz and Guildenstern as separate entities?

4.

Polonius is usually played as a figure of fun, a doddering old fool. Yet he has been clever enough to survive as first minister to Old Hamlet and

[margin note: what does this tell us of Hamlet?]

Claudius, no mean tight-rope feat, so perhaps Peter Hall was right to see him as 'the kind of tough, shrewd establishment figure you can still meet in St. James's; a man who sends himself up and uses his silly humour as a weapon.' If you were producing *Hamlet*, what direction would you give to the actor playing Polonius?

It is interesting to note that, although Hamlet is peculiarly diffident about killing Claudius, the deaths of Polonius and Rosencrantz and Guildenstern bring out a show of callousness in him. Why is this? Do you agree with Hamlet's instant character sketches over Polonius's body?

5.

Hamlet is predominantly disillusioned and cynical. Perhaps the only time in the play when he refrains from cynicism is in the description of his father in I 2 and III 4. Contrast the idealistic (?) portrait of Old Hamlet with the vilification of Claudius on these two occasions. Can the descriptions be accepted at their face value?

6.

In V 2 Hamlet says, referring to the dispatch of Rosencrantz and Guildenstern,

> 'Tis dangerous when the baser nature comes
> Between the pass and fell-incensèd points
> Of mighty opposites.

How do you see Claudius in this play? Do you think of Hamlet and Claudius as the clash of two "mighty opposites"?

Every time Hamlet speaks of Claudius, it is in the most violent language indicative of deep disgust of the worst villain that ever smiled in Denmark. Examine the appropriate passages and consider whether your view of Claudius coincides with Hamlet's.

7.

Although most people find *Hamlet* a fascinating play and are happy to accept that somehow or other it is a considerable work of art, T. S. Eliot once saw fit to describe it as an "artistic failure". He thought that all Hamlet's disgust and disillusionment stem largely from his mother's infidelity to Old Hamlet's memory by her "o'er-hasty marriage" to Claudius. Yet, he felt that the character of Gertrude is not such as to inspire this deep emotion; she is perhaps too insignificant, insufficiently developed. This he regarded as a weakness in the play.

Examine your attitude to Gertrude and her part in the play; and consider how far you sympathise with Eliot's point of view.

OTHER CHARACTERS

8.

Occasionally, productions of *Hamlet* omit Fortinbras altogether. By examining the places where Fortinbras occurs, say what you consider are the problems involved in omitting him from the play and evaluate especially what effect his absence would have on the end of the play. Bear in mind that in excluding Fortinbras from the final scene, you are affecting the relevance of the soliloquy, "How all occasions do inform against me."

If you were directing *Hamlet* and had decided to dispense with Fortinbras, how would you end the play? What reasons would you give for leaving him out? How would you justify your ending?

9.

There are many ghosts in Shakespeare, but the ghost in *Hamlet* is unique.

Examine some of the other Shakespearian ghosts, for example in *Richard III, Macbeth, Julius Caesar,* and compare them with the spirit of Old Hamlet.

Without doubt, the ghost's earlier appearances are objective (i.e. they are seen by several people) but in the later bedroom scene Gertrude cannot see the apparition and calls it the "coinage" of Hamlet's brain. Comment on this.

One of the problems of producing *Hamlet* on the stage is to gain credibility for the ghost. Mr. Wopsle's production in Chapter 31 of *Great Expectations* would not be classed as one of the most successful interpretations of the ghost. If you were producing *Hamlet*, how would you present the ghost?

10.

When we first see Hamlet greet Horatio, the impression is gained that they have not met for some time even though they have both been in Denmark for more than two months (I 2 160 ff), behaviour not indicative of close friendship. Yet by the end of the play, Horatio is willing to take poison in order to join Hamlet in death. Examine their relationship and consider whether the development is plausible.

Sometimes, when we make an armchair study of a play, discrepancies appear which we would scarcely notice in the theatre. Is this in any way true of Horatio?

Themes and Dramatic Design

1.

Hamlet has been described as a play full of questions with very few answers. Some of these questions are listed below. Examine the passages in which they occur and say what light they shed on the nature of the play:

a) . . . to me, what is this quintessence of dust?   II 2 311

b) What should such fellows as I do crawling between earth and heaven?   III 1 128

c) What is a man,
   If his chief good and market of his time
   Be but to sleep and feed?   IV 4 33

d) How long will a man lie i'th' earth ere he rot?   V 1 158

e) Am I a coward?   II 2 574

2.

Because Shakespeare was writing at a time when Christianity was the prevailing belief amongst his audience, many of his plays take place within a Christian framework. Nevertheless, the dominant atmosphere of the majority of Shakespeare's tragedies has little to do with Christianity: the feeling is generally one of man facing a vast universe (rarely benevolent like the Christian concept of the Godhead) as nobly as he can. List the Christian references in *Hamlet* and consider whether the prevailing atmosphere of the play is in tune with them.

You might like to consider the following: comments by the ghost and what other characters say about the ghost; Hamlet's first soliloquy in I 2; Claudius's prayer and Hamlet's reasons for not killing his uncle in III 3; Hamlet's comments on the dead Polonius in IV 3; the burial of Ophelia in V 1; Horatio's speech to the dead Hamlet in V 2.

3.

Many of the questions in *Hamlet* are concerned with what happens to us, body and soul, after death. Examine the passages where such questions are formulated and deduce what you can about the Elizabethan attitude to death and its consequences.

You might like to consider the following: the evidence of the ghost; Hamlet's soliloquy in III 1; the king's prayer in III 3; Hamlet's speculation on the condition of the dead Polonius in IV 7; the graveyard scene; Horatio's panegyric over Hamlet in V 2.

4.

In Greek tragedy, Fate was seen to play a significant part. In Shakespearian tragedy, by contrast, character can be said to predominate over destiny.

Examine the following references to Providence and divine influence in *Hamlet*:

> and that should learn us   V 2 9
> There's a divinity that shapes our ends,
> Rough-hew them how we will,

together with:

> There is special providence in the fall of a sparrow   V 2 217

and:

> Our wills and fates do so contrary run,   III 2 210
> That our devices still are overthrown,
> Our thoughts are ours, their ends none of our own . . . .

Discuss the extent of the role of Fate in the play.

5.

Examine the use of the word "conscience" as it occurs in the following passages and consider what light it sheds on the meaning of the play:

a)   The play's the thing   II 2 609
Wherein I'll catch the conscience of the king.

b) How smart a lash that speech doth give my conscience!   III 1 50

c) Thus conscience doth make cowards of us all.   III 1 83

d) Now must your conscience my acquittance seal   IV 7 1

e) They are not near my conscience   V 2 58

f)   Is't not perfect conscience
   To quit him with this arm?

g) And yet 'tis almost 'gainst my conscience   V 2 294

6.

In every Shakespearian play there are passages which seem to be of great importance as an indication of the nature of the play, although they may not always be obvious in their meaning. Consider the following lines in their context and discuss what you think is their implication:

a) The time is out of joint; O cursèd spite   I 5 187
   That ever I was born to set it right!

b) Our indiscretion sometimes serves us well   V 2 8
   When our deep plots do pall; and that should learn us
   There's a divinity that shapes our ends,
   Rough-hew them how we will.

c) Not a whit, we defy augury; there's a special   V 2 217
   providence in the fall of a sparrow. If it be now,
   'tis not to come; if it be not to come, it will be now;
   if it be not now, yet it will come: the readiness is all.

7.

It was common practice in Shakespeare's day for playwrights to use their plays as vehicles for criticism of other authors and of actors, theatres and audiences. In *Hamlet* many lines are devoted to conversation involving the players. From a reading of these passages, what can you deduce about the contemporary theatre and Shakespeare's views on it?

8.

If you were directing *Hamlet*, which aspects of the play would you emphasise to indicate its relevance to a modern audience?
   Here are some possible angles for you to consider:
a) Standards of morality have fallen so low that the man of integrity can no longer identify himself with society.
b) Politics have lost the art of social welfare and substituted the grasp of power for its own sake.
c) The future looks so bleak that it seems pointless trying to do anything about it.
d) The man with sensitivity is out of tune with society in general.

9.

Every clown, we are told, is ambitious to play Hamlet, and the play itself is still the most frequently performed and studied work in the world.

THEMES AND DRAMATIC DESIGN

It appeals to all races and all temperaments in all ages. Have you personally found anything in the play which you think might account for this universality and timelessness?

10.

Discuss what you consider to be the function of the opening scene of a play, and what qualities are best suited to fulfilling that function.

Read some other opening scenes in Shakespeare, for example *Julius Caesar, Henry V, King Lear*, and in the light of this experience evaluate the opening scene(s) of *Hamlet*.

11.

The gravediggers' scene is often simply dismissed as comic relief from the intensity and gloominess of the tragedy, a kind of sop for the 'groundlings' who might perhaps have been made restive by the static nature of the play.

There is undoubtedly some truth in this: it is never wise to forget that Shakespeare's playhouse was a very different place from our polite theatres with everyone packed harmlessly in rows. It had to compete with the more vulgar pastimes of bear-baiting and cock-fighting, and existed in a more boisterously critical atmosphere (read the appropriate parts of 'Life in Shakespeare's England' by John Dover Wilson). If Shakespeare's plays failed to intrigue the audience, then his theatre would not have been a paying proposition.

Nevertheless, Shakespeare rarely introduces comic material purely for entertainment – you may remember that in III 2 of *Hamlet* he criticises those clowns who ad lib. to the bawdier part of the audience and thereby delay the progress of the play's main action. The 'comic' or 'low' scenes in Shakespeare will usually have some bearing on the overall themes of the play. Do you think that the gravediggers' scene is closely relevant to the main part of *Hamlet?*

12.

In the years which preceded the staging of *Hamlet*, the revenge tragedies so popular in the Elizabethan theatre were not really tragedies at all; they were melodrama. This is to say that rather than being concerned with gaining sympathy for the hero's condition of life, they set out merely to excite, intrigue and thrill the audience in much the same way as a modern murder film.

Although *Hamlet* has progressed from pure melodrama into what we call tragedy, it still contains many elements which to an Elizabethan audience would appear melodramatic.

Discuss what it is that distinguishes a melodrama from a tragedy.

Identify the aspects and incidents of *Hamlet* which you think might have been appropriate in an earlier melodrama. Consider whether any of these seem at all out of place in the present tragedy.

13.

It has been said that *Hamlet* is weak in terms of construction, and that particularly there is a flatness and dullness about the play during the time when Hamlet is on his voyage to England. Evaluate what happens during Hamlet's absence and say whether or not you feel that the interest of the action lapses at this stage.

14.

Most of Shakespeare's plays follow their source material more or less closely. Examine the sources from which Shakespeare took the Hamlet story, identify the elements of *Hamlet* which are taken from those sources and consider how Shakespeare has incorporated and changed them.

It has been suggested that by including source material which proved indigestible or intractable Shakespeare has made *Hamlet* defective in terms of the clear development of some of its characters and relationships, e.g. the relationship between Hamlet and Ophelia, Hamlet's "madness".

By examining the use which Shakespeare has made of his source material, is it possible to deduce anything about Shakespeare's interests in his play?

15.

It is a commonplace of Shakespearian criticism that Shakespeare was more concerned with character than plot, and it has been said of *Hamlet* that its plot creaks. Examine the story and its progress and say what weaknesses you can find. Are any of them due to a failure properly to absorb source material? Would they be noticed in the theatre?

16.

Dr. Johnson said that *Hamlet* was characterised by "variety". Make a list of all the separate incidents in the play and consider how many of them make progress towards the climax of the play.

Can you justify the inclusion of the other incidents in terms of character, atmosphere, theme or special interest?

Do you consider the action of the play to be diffuse?

THEMES AND DRAMATIC DESIGN

Language, Expression and Style

I.

Hamlet offers a surprising variety of style. Examine each of the following passages and, considering the appropriateness of its expression to the speaker and the circumstances in which the passage is spoken, comment upon its style:

a) If thou hast any sound or use of voice,   I I 128
   Speak to me.
   If there be any good thing to be done
   That may to thee do ease, and grace to me,
   Speak to me.
   If thou art privy to thy country's fate
   Which happily foreknowing may avoid,
   O, speak!
   Or if thou hast uphoarded in thy life
   Extorted treasure in the womb of earth,
   For which they say you spirits oft walk in death,
   Speak of it – stay and speak – stop it, Marcellus!

b) Though yet of Hamlet our dear brother's death   I 2 I
   The memory be green, and that it us befitted
   To bear our hearts in grief, and our whole kingdom
   To be contracted in one brow of woe,
   Yet so far hath discretion fought with nature,
   That we with wisest sorrow think on him
   Together with remembrance of ourselves:
   Therefore our sometime sister, now our queen,
   Th'imperial jointress to this warlike state,
   Have we as 'twere with a defeated joy,
   With an auspicious, and a dropping eye,
   With mirth in funeral, and with dirge in marriage,
   In equal scale weighing delight and dole,
   Taken to wife: nor have we herein barred
   Your better wisdoms, which have freely gone
   With this affair along – for all, our thanks.

c) O, what a noble mind is here o'erthrown!   III 1 153
   The courtier's, soldier's, scholar's, eye, tongue, sword,
   Th'expectancy and rose of the fair state,
   The glass of fashion, and the mould of form,
   Th'observed of all observers, quite quite down,
   And I of ladies most deject and wretched,
   That sucked the honey of his music vows,
   Now see that noble and most sovereign reason
   Like sweet bells jangled, out of tune and harsh,
   That unmatched form and feature of blown youth,
   Blasted with ecstasy!

d) O all you host of heaven! O earth! what else?   I 5 92
   And shall I couple hell? O fie! Hold, hold, my heart,
   And you, my sinews, grow not instant old,
   But bear me stiffly up . . . Remember thee?
   Ay thou poor ghost whiles memory holds a seat
   In this distracted globe. Remember thee?
   Yea, from the table of my memory
   I'll wipe away all trivial fond records,
   All saws of books, all forms, all pressures past
   That youth and observation copied there,
   And thy commandment all alone shall live
   Within the book and volume of my brain,
   Unmixed with baser matter – yes by heaven!
   O most pernicious woman!
   O villain, villain, smiling, damnéd villain!
   My tables, meet it is I set it down
   That one may smile, and smile, and be a villain,
   At least I am sure it may be so in Denmark . . .

e) Polonius: My liege and madam, to expostulate   II 2 86
          What majesty should be, what duty is,
          Why day is day, night night, and time is time,
          Were nothing but to waste night, day and time.
          Therefore since brevity is the soul of wit,
          And tediousness the limbs and outward flourishes,
          I will be brief – you noble son is mad:
          Mad call I it, for to define true madness,
          What is't but to be nothing else but mad?
          But let that go.
   Queen: More matter, with less art.
   Polonius: Madam, I swear I use no art at all.
          That he is mad 'tis true, 'tis true, 'tis pity,
          And pity 'tis 'tis true – a foolish figure,

But farewell it, for I will use no art.
Mad let us grant him then, and now remains
That we find out the cause of this effect,
Or rather say, the cause of this defect,
For this effect defective comes by cause:
Thus it remains, and the remainder thus.

f) I have of late, but wherefore I know not, lost all my   II 2 299
mirth, forgone all custom of exercises: and indeed it
goes so heavily with my disposition, that this goodly
frame the earth, seems to me a sterile promontory,
this most excellent canopy the air, look you, this
brave o'erhanging firmament, this majestical roof
fretted with golden fire, why it appeareth nothing
to me but a foul and pestilent congregation of
vapours . . . What a piece of work is a man, how
noble in reason, how infinite in faculties, in form
and moving, how express and admirable in action,
how like an angel in apprehension, how like a god:
the beauty of the world; the paragon of animals;
and yet to me, what is this quintessence of dust?

g) 'The rugged Pyrrhus, he whose sable arms,   II 2 456
Black as his purpose, did the night resemble
When he lay couchéd in th'ominous horse,
Hath now this dread and black complexion smeared
With heraldy more dismal: head to foot
Now is he total gules, horridly tricked
With blood of fathers, mothers, daughters, sons,
Baked and impasted with the parching streets,
That lend a tyrannous and a damnéd light
To their lord's murder. Roasted in wrath and fire,
And thus o'er-sizéd with coagulate gore,
With eyes like carbuncles, the hellish Pyrrhus
Old grandsire Priam seeks' . . .

h) There is a willow grows askant the brook,
That shows his hoar leaves in the glassy stream,
Therewith fantastic garlands did she make
Of crow-flowers, nettles, daisies, and long purples
That liberal shepherds give a grosser name,
But our cold maids do dead men's fingers call them.
There on the pendent boughs her crownet weeds
Clamb'ring to hang, an envious sliver broke,

When down her weedy trophies and herself
Fell in the weeping brook. Her clothes spread wide,
And mermaid-like awhile they bore her up,
Which time she chanted snatches of old lauds,
As one incapable of her own distress,
Or like a creature native and indued
Unto that element. But long it could not be
Till that her garments, heavy with their drink,
Pulled the poor wretch from her melodious lay
To muddy death.

i) This world is not for aye, nor 'tis not strange   III 2 199
That even our loves should with our fortunes change:
For 'tis a question left us yet to prove,
Whether love lead fortune, or else fortune love.
The great man down, you mark his favourite flies,
The poor advanced makes friends of enemies,
And hitherto doth love on fortune tend,
For who not needs shall never lack a friend,
And who in want a hollow friend doth try,
Directly seasons him his enemy.
But orderly to end where I begun,
Our wills and fates do so contrary run,
That our devices still are overthrown,
Our thoughts are ours, their ends none of our own –
So think thou wilt no second husband wed,
But die thy thoughts when thy first lord is dead.

j) 'Swounds, show me what thou't do: V 1 268
Woo't weep? woo't fight? woo't fast? woo't tear thyself?
Woo't drink up eisel? eat a crocodile?
I'll do't. Dost thou come here to whine?
To outface me with leaping in her grave?
Be buried quick with her, and so will I.
And if thou prate of mountains, let them throw
Millions of acres on us, till our ground,
Singeing his pate against the burning zone,
Make Ossa like a wart! nay, an thou'lt mouth,
I'll rant as well as thou.

2.

Hamlet spends an unusual amount of his time speaking in soliloquy.
Explain the purpose of this theatrical device; say why it is useful, and
why it is particularly suited to Hamlet's situation.
  Are there disadvantages to the soliloquy?

LANGUAGE, EXPRESSION AND STYLE

Suppose that you were Shakespeare and you had decided to omit one of the major soliloquies. Which one would you cut out and what would you put in its place to serve a similar purpose?

3.

Examine I 3 and II 1. These scenes may seem rather long drawn-out in proportion to the importance of their content. How important and necessary are they as scenes? Could you say, perhaps, that parts are essential whilst others could be dispensed with? Is there a good reason for retaining them as they are?

4.

With the idea of the play-within-the-play already conceived in his mind, Hamlet says to the player in II 2 – "You could, for a need, study a speech of some dozen or sixteen lines, which I would set down and insert in it, could you not?" Presuming that Shakespeare carried through Hamlet's intention, which lines in the ensuing play do you think are the inserted ones?

5.

Quote three passages from the play (they need not be long ones) which have struck you by the beauty of their poetry. Comment on them and say why, in a play largely occupied with cynicism, such passages should occur at those points.

6.

From time to time Shakespeare has been re-written by various purists who found him too vigorous and crude for the palate of their delicate age. The following passage is an example: it is a "less offensive" version of the "To be or not to be" soliloquy. Contrast the two passages by examining a) their different attitudes towards death and the after-life, and b) the changes in diction. Try to deduce the author's purpose in re-writing the passage.

Consider which passage is superior as poetry. Can you pin down the reasons for your choice?

> A. My anxious soul is torn with doubtful strife,
> And hangs suspended betwixt death and life;
> Life! death! dread objects of mankind's debate;
> Whether superior to the shocks of fate,
> To bear its fiercest ills with steadfast mind,
> To Nature's order piously resign'd
> Or, with magnanimous and brave disdain,
> Return her back th'injurious gift again.
> O! if to die, this mortal bustle o'er,

Were but to close one's eyes, and be no more;
From pain, from sickness, sorrows, safe withdrawn,
In night eternal that shall know no dawn;
This dread, imperial, wond'rous frame of man,
Lost in still nothing, whence it first began:
Yes, if the grave such quiet could supply,
Devotion's self might even dare to die.
But fearful here, though curious to explore,
Thought pauses, trembling on the hither shore,
Lest, hapless victors in the mortal strife,
Through death we struggle but to second life.
What scenes may rise, awake the human fear;
Being again resum'd, and God more near;
If awful thunders the new guest appal,
Or the soft voice of gentle mercy call.
This teaches life with all its ills to please,
Afflicting poverty, severe disease;
To lowest infamy gives power to charm,
And strikes the dagger from the boldest arm.

B. To be, or not to be, that is the question . . .   III I 56
   to . . . lose the name of action.   III I 88

7.

Shakespeare often indicated the themes running through his plays by means of recurring imagery. How far is it helpful towards an understanding of *Hamlet* to examine its dominant imagery of disease and hypocrisy?

Ophelia is associated with flowers. Examine the appropriate passages (her mad scene, IV 5; the queen's announcement of her death in IV 7; her burial in V 1) and comment on the use of this flower imagery.

Passages for Comment

1.

Frailty, thy name is woman!
A little month or ere those shoes were old
With which she followed my poor father's body
Like Niobe all tears, why she, even she –
5 O God, a beast that wants discourse of reason
Would have mourned longer – married with mine uncle,
My father's brother, but no more like my father
Than I to Hercules; within a month,
Ere yet the salt of most unrighteous tears
10 Had left the flushing in her gallèd eyes,
She married. O most wicked speed, to post
With such dexterity to incestuous sheets!
It is not, nor it cannot come to good.

1) Say by whom and in what circumstances this passage is spoken.
2) Comment on the speaker's state of mind and the reasons for it.
3) How does the style of the passage reflect the speaker's state of mind?
4) Explain and comment on
   a) Frailty, thy name is woman
   b) Like Niobe, all tears
   c) To post with such dexterity to incestuous sheets

2.

Was your father dear to you?
Or are you like the *painting of a sorrow*,
A face without a heart?
Not that I think you did not love your father,
5 But that I know love is begun by time,
And that I see, in passages of proof,
Time qualifies the spark and fire of it.
There lives within the very flame of love
A kind of wick or snuff that will abate it,
10 And nothing is at a like goodness still,
For goodness, *growing to a plurisy*,
Dies in his own too-much. That we would do,

We should do when we would, for this 'would' changes,
15 And hath abatements and delays as many
As there are tongues, are hands, are accidents;
And then this 'should' is like a spendthrift sigh,
That hurts by easing. But, *to the quick o'the ulcer;*

1) Say by whom and in what circumstances this passage is spoken.
2) How does this passage relate to the themes of the play?
3) Comment on the images italicised in the passage and discuss their significance to the play as a whole.

3.

I'll tent him to the quick: if a' do blench
I know my course. The spirit that I have seen
May be a devil: and the devil hath power
T'assume a pleasing shape, yea, and perhaps
5 Out of my weakness and my melancholy
As he is very potent with such spirits
Abuses me to damn me. I'll have grounds
More relative than this: the play's the thing
Wherein I'll catch the conscience of the king.

1) Say by whom and in what circumstances this passage is spoken.
2) Narrate the passage in your own words so as to bring out the meaning.
3) Relate the present thoughts of the speaker in the passage to his thoughts about the ghost in I 5.
4) In terms of what later happens in the play, comment on the first lines of this passage – "I'll tent him to the quick: if a' do blench I know my course."
5) Comment on the word "melancholy".
6) Why do you think the last two lines rhyme?

4.

Alas, poor Yorick. I knew him, Horatio; a fellow of
infinite jest, of most excellent fancy; he hath borne
me on his back a thousand times; and now, how
abhorred in my imagination it is! my gorge rises at
5 it. Here hung those lips that I have kissed I know
not how oft. Where be your jibes now? your
gambols? your songs? your flashes of merriment,
that were wont to set the table on a roar? Not one
now, to mock your own grinning? quite chapfallen?
10 Now get you to my lady's chamber and tell her,
let her paint an inch thick, to this favour she must
come; make her laugh at that.

1) Say by whom and in what circumstances this passage is spoken.
2) Who was Yorick?
3) What light does this passage cast on the state of Hamlet's mind?
4) Explain "to my lady's chamber and tell her, let her paint an inch thick, to this favour she must come; make her laugh at that." Can you recall any other passages from the play where the use of cosmetics is mentioned?

5.

Haste me to know't, that I, with wings as swift
As meditation or the thoughts of love,
May sweep to my revenge.
　　　　　　　I find thee apt,
And duller shouldst thou be than the fat weed
5 That rots itself in ease on Lethe wharf
Wouldst thou not stir in this.

1) Say by whom and in what circumstances this passage is spoken.
2) Both of the speakers in this extract might fairly be accused of unconscious irony. Explain why.
3) Comment on the image in lines 1–3 ("with wings . . . my revenge").
4) Comment on the image in lines 4–5 ("fat weed . . . Lethe wharf").

6.

Since my dear soul was mistress of her choice
And could of men distinguish her election,
Sh'hath seal'd thee for herself; for thou hast been
As one in suff'ring all that suffers nothing,
5 A man that Fortune's buffets and rewards
Hast ta'en with equal thanks; and blest are those
Whose blood and judgment are so well co-medled
That they are not a pipe for Fortune's finger
To sound what stop she please: give me that man
10 That is not passion's slave, and I will wear him
In my heart's core, ay, in my heart of heart,
As I do thee.

1) Say by whom and in what circumstances the passage is spoken.
2) Who in the play might best fit the description "passion's slave"? Account for your choice.
3) The speaker obviously admires the person to whom he is speaking. What does he admire about him? What particular reason has the speaker for admiring this quality?
4) The word "fortune" is used here twice. It is also used elsewhere in the play in the phrase, "the slings and arrows of outrageous fortune." Is

there any connection between the two passages?

5) The image of playing on a pipe or recorder is used again at another part of the play. Can you say where?

6) What is meant by
    a) "could of men distinguish"
    b) "blest are those whose blood and judgement are so well co-medled."

7.

'Swounds, show me what thou'lt do:
Woo't weep? woo't fight? woo't fast? woo't tear thyself?
Woo't drink up eisel? eat a crocodile?
I'll do't. Dost thou come here to whine?
5 To outface me by leaping in her grave?
Be buried quick with her, and so will I.
And if thou prate of mountains, let them throw
Millions of acres on us, till our ground,
Singeing his pate against the burning zone,
10 Make Ossa like a wart! Nay an thou'lt mouth,
I'll rant as well as thou.

1) Say by whom and in what circumstances this passage is spoken.
2) Relate the style of the passage to the mood of the speaker.
3) Look up the word "hyperbole" in a good dictionary and comment on it in relation to this passage.
'4) Would you consider
    a) the language of the passage and
    b) the action which accompanies it to be characteristic of the speaker?

8.

'Tis now the very witching time of night,
When churchyards yawn and hell itself breathes out
Contagion to this world: now could I drink hot blood
And do such bitter business as the day
5 Would quake to look on: soft, now to my mother –
O heart! lose not thy nature; let not ever
The soul of Nero enter this firm bosom;
Let me be cruel, not unnatural;
I will speak daggers to her, but use none.

1) Say by whom and in what circumstances this passage is spoken.
2) Explain and comment, in terms of the character of the speaker, on the phrase "Now could I drink hot blood." Does it recall any other passage of the play?
3) Explain
    a) O heart lose not thy nature

b) The soul of Nero
c) I will speak daggers to her.

9.

Now might I do it pat, now a' is a-praying;
And now I'll do't: and so he goes to heaven;
And so I am revenged. That would be scanned:
A villain kills my father; and for that,
5 I, his sole son, do this same villain send
To heaven.
Why, this is bait and salary, not revenge.
He took my father grossly, full of bread,
With all his crimes broad blown, as flush as May.

1) Say by whom and in what circumstance this passage is spoken.
2) Explain the significance of the passage in terms of
   a) the character of the speaker
   b) what happens soon afterwards.

10.

'Swounds, I should take it, for it cannot be
But I am pigeon-livered, and lack gall
To make oppression bitter, or ere this
I should ha' fatted all the region kites
5 With this slave's offal. Bloody, bawdy villain!
Remorseless, treacherous, lecherous, kindless villain!
O, vengeance!
Why, what an ass am I. This is most brave
That I, the son of a dear father murdered,
10 Prompted to my revenge by heaven and hell,
Must like a whore unpack my heart with words.

1) Say by whom and in what circumstances the passage is spoken.
2) How does the style of the passage reflect the speaker's state of mind?
3) What light does the passage throw on the character of the speaker?

11.

And with a sudden vigour it doth posset
And curd, like eager droppings into milk
The thin and wholesome blood: so did it mine;
And a most instant tetter bark'd about,
5 Most lazar-like, with vile and loathsome crust,
All my smooth body.
Thus was I . . . .
Cut off even in the blossoms of my sin,
Unhousel'd, disappointed, unanel'd.

1) Say by whom and in what circumstances this passage is spoken.
2) In terms of the play, could the passage have a symbolic as well as a literal significance?
3) Explain lines 7–9. Do these lines have any effect on the later progress of the play?

        12.
    This is the very ecstasy of love,
    Whose violent property fordoes itself
    And leads the will to desperate undertakings
    As oft as any passion under heaven
  5 That does afflict our natures.
    . . . .
    I am sorry that with better heed and judgement
    I had not quoted him.

1) Say by whom and in what circumstances this passage is spoken.
2) What light does the passage cast upon the character of the speaker?
3) In terms of what happens in the play, comment on the phrase "ecstasy of love."

        13.
              For love of grace,
    Lay not that flattering unction to your soul,
    That not your trespass but my madness speaks,
    It will but skin and film the ulcerous place,
  5 Whiles rank corruption mining all within,
    Infects unseen. Confess yourself to heaven;
    Repent what's past; avoid what is to come;
    And do not spread the compost on the weeds
    To make them ranker.

1) Say by whom and in what circumstances this passage is spoken.
2) With reference to the play, comment on the phrase 'my madness speaks.'
3) Discuss the imagery of this passage and relate it to any similar imagery in other parts of the play. Does the imagery have any bearing on the themes of the play?

130

Appendix 1

Aristotle and Shakespeare

No one can progress far in the study of *Hamlet* or any Shakespearian tragedy without becoming aware that Aristotle incorporated in his *Poetics* some opinions on the nature of Greek tragedy which seem to intrude into every discussion on the subject of tragedy in any age. About the influence exerted by Aristotle's words there can be no doubt: at times his definition has been forced on dramatists like a strait-jacket; Shakespeare himself has been condemned for writing "un-classical" tragedies; and, as late as this century, Arthur Miller was astonished to find himself criticized by the academic purists for creating, in Willy Loman in *Death of a Salesman*, a non-Aristotelian tragic hero.

Unfortunately, although Aristotle's influence is clear enough, the meaning of parts of his "definition" is less so. Debate has been long and inconclusive. For that reason it seemed preferable to adopt an uncomplicated line in the body of the book (see Page 26) in order not to interrupt the flow of argument, and to defer discussion to this appendix.

The main question arises over the meaning we attach to the word *hamartia* as it was used in the *Poetics*. Aristotle suggests that the tragic hero is a basically good man who falls from initial prosperity to degradation and ultimate death because of *hamartia*. This was taken by the Victorian critics to denote a moral flaw or fault, a weakness or an excess in the hero's make-up which somehow overwhelmed his otherwise sound character and brought about the tragedy. This concept of *hamartia* was found convenient for examining Shakespeare's tragedies: Othello was credulous and prone to jealousy, and was accordingly driven to kill the innocent Desdemona; Lear was vain and lacking in self-knowledge, and consequently placed himself in a position where he could be maltreated and maddened by his "dog-hearted" daughters; Antony became so infatuated with Cleopatra that he neglected and lost an empire; Brutus's political naiveté caused him to be manipulated by an unscrupulous man.

Although this meaning of *hamartia* is apparently convenient for elucidating Shakespearean tragedy, it may be somewhat removed from Aristotle's intention in using the word because, generally speaking, Shakespeare's heroes have more control over their destiny than did the heroes of Greek tragedy. Greek scholars are divided about the word's meaning in its Aristotelian context. In any case, the "moral flaw" interpretation of *hamartia* is only doubtfully helpful vis-à-vis Shakespeare because to emphasise that downfall is directly attributable to a fault suggests the adoption of a moral tone. In other words, we ought to take from *Antony and Cleopatra* the message that, if Antony had possessed more self-control, he would have remained one of the leaders of the Roman world and all would have been well. Now, without doubt, there is a strong tradition of morality behind Elizabethan drama, but to see Shakespeare in terms of a moral dramatist is too unsubtle. In Shakespeare's tragedies humanity is the important note: Mark Antony's commendation of Brutus at the close of *Julius Caesar* could serve as an epitaph to every Shakespearian tragic hero:

> This was the noblest Roman of them all.
> All the conspirators save only he
> Did that they did in envy of great Caesar;
> He only in a general honest thought
> And common good to all made one of them.
> His life was gentle; all the elements
> So mixed in him that Nature might stand up
> And say to all the world 'This was a man!'

Brutus's naiveté may have led to disillusionment, but we do not wish him any different; Antony may have lost an empire because of his unbridled sensual attraction to Cleopatra, but he means more to us as a man than does his calculating partner, Octavius.

This fatal-flaw interpretation of *hamartia* is even less applicable to Hamlet as a tragic hero. Jealousy, pride, ambition, vanity leading to catastrophe; these we can conceive and perhaps accept in the terms of the moralist; but what exactly is Hamlet's weakness or fatal flaw? It is something to do with a diffidence about killing for revenge, and, morally speaking, that must be considered a doubtful fault. Consequently, an approach to *Hamlet* along these lines must be questionable. To explain the catastrophe which overwhelms Hamlet, we ought to look less towards character fault and more towards a consideration of the problem of evil in the world, that good men often cause suffering by the most well-meaning actions.

Nevertheless, we would do well to include the fatal flaw in our thinking about *Hamlet* as a tragedy (despite its being generally discredited) if only because the idea lingers on. When Olivier directed his film version of *Hamlet* in 1948, he emphasised the fatal-flaw approach by prefacing the action with the speech beginning:

> So, oft it chances in particular men,
> That for some vicious mole of nature in them . . .

He saw *Hamlet* as the tragedy of a man who could not make up his mind.

Appendix 2

A Guide to some useful publications

A. C. BRADLEY: *SHAKESPEARIAN TRAGEDY* (MACMILLAN AND CO. LTD) 1905

A giant of Shakespearian criticism, its exposition of the plays by means of analysis of the characters, almost at times as if they were real people, is a culmination of the ninteenth century approach of Lamb, Hazlitt and Coleridge. An indication of Bradley's influence on Shakespeare studies is given in this rhyme by Guy Boas:

> I dreamt last night that Shakespeare's ghost
> Sat for a Civil Service post.
> The English papers of the year
> Contained a question on *King Lear*,
> Which Shakespeare answered rather badly
> Because he hadn't studied Bradley.

And even today, seventy years later, university dons complain that sixthformers seem not to get beyond Bradley.

Perhaps because of its eminence the book became something of an Aunt Sally for the next generation of critics, and for a time it was ignored. More recently, however, it has emerged, its paintwork a bit chipped but structurally intact, to enjoy something of a revival; and rightly so, for Bradley writes for the most part with sanity and insight and the simplicity of phrase which characterizes a good teacher.

The first two chapters deal with the nature of Shakespearian tragedy in general and these are followed by two chapters on each of *Hamlet*, *Othello*, *King Lear* and *Macbeth*.

This is essential and interesting reading. Even if, for the sake of the dons, you make a mental note to progress past Bradley, from the point of view of your own foundation you cannot afford to ignore him.

J. DOVER WILSON: *WHAT HAPPENS IN HAMLET* (CAMBRIDGE UNIVERSITY PRESS) 1951

An excellent example of one type of reaction against (or extension of) Bradleian criticism: the historical or back-to-the-Elizabethans approach. Dover Wilson tries to emphasize those aspects of character and drama which would have been evident to Shakespeare's contemporary audience but which might elude us. He uses his textual expertise (he is one of the editors of The New Cambridge Shakespeare) to shed more light on the antic disposition, the nature of the ghost, the effect of Gertrude's behaviour on Hamlet, and the precise significance of the obscurities in the play scene.

Like Bradley, Dover Wilson puts life into scholarship.

G. WILSON KNIGHT: *THE WHEEL OF FIRE* 1930 AND *THE IMPERIAL THEME* 1931 (METHUEN AND CO LTD.) 1951

One of the founding fathers of a school of criticism reacting against the Bradleian approach through character, he is concerned with what he calls the Shakespearian progress (i.e. the interpretation of the plays in relation to one another); and he analyses the plays through their poetic symbolism or imaginative design (e.g. he detects the opposition of life and death forces in the tragedies). Character is subordinated to poetic meaning.

The essays on *Hamlet* in these two books are only a small part of Knight's attempt to provide a continuous interpretation of the main body of Shakespeare's work. *Hamlet, Embassy of Death* (in *The Wheel of Fire*) is interesting in that it sees Hamlet almost as the villain to the play.

Although Wilson Knight's approach is probably of no more intrinsic value than Bradley's, it has occupied the energies of many of the best critics of the middle part of this century.

L. C. KNIGHTS: *AN APPROACH TO HAMLET* (CHATTO AND WINDUS LTD) 1960

Knights has been influenced by Wilson Knight but has a greater awareness of the pitfalls of the exclusively symbolic approach to Shakespeare: "a preoccupation with imagery and symbols (Wilson Knight!), unless minutely controlled by a sensitive intelligence directed upon the text, can lead to abstractions almost as dangerous as does a preoccupation with character (Bradley!)." The title of one of L. C. Knights' essays, *How Many Children Had Lady Macbeth?*, has been used as a label of scorn to represent the worst excesses of the 'character' school which tried to give the characters a real existence beyond the scope of the plays.

An Approach to Hamlet provides a good balance of the historical, the character and the thematic/symbolic attitudes.

HARRY LEVIN: *THE QUESTION OF HAMLET* (OXFORD UNIVERSITY PRESS) 1959.

Like Knights and Wilson Knight, Levin is concerned with the thematic continuity of the play and examines it through its verbal echoes and complexities. As the title suggests, Levin finds that the air of questioning and mystery which characterises criticism of this play is a reflection of the play's own structure.

This book makes the student aware of the richness of the text.

HARLEY GRANVILLE-BARKER: *PREFACES TO SHAKESPEARE; THIRD SERIES; HAMLET*, 1930 (SIDGWICK AND JACKSON) 1937

Granville-Barker is the most famous of the theatre-minded critics of this century. With experiences as a playwright and a producer he has attempted a balanced approach which examines Shakespeare's design and characterisation through his stagecraft. Although he leans on Bradley, his endeavours to keep the demands of the stage-production always in mind provide a useful antidote to the sometimes remote psychological approach.

T. S. ELIOT: *SELECTED ESSAYS* (FABER AND FABER)

Eliot's short essay, *Hamlet* (1919) is famous because, in cavalier fashion, it dares to call the play an artistic failure (cf. Page 44). It has provoked considerable discussion.

ERNEST JONES: *HAMLET AND OEDIPUS* (VICTOR GOLLANCZ LTD) 1949

The psychoanalysts have found lots of material in Shakespeare's plays and, not surprisingly, the eccentric Hamlet has proved the most popular case. Among a bevy of indifferent or ridiculous studies of this kind, Ernest Jones' book stands more reasonably, or at least chapters 3 and 4 do. Jones psychoanalyses Hamlet to probe his motives for delay and reaches the conclusion that they lie too deep in his subconscious for him to realise or understand. If Hamlet cannot fathom his own springs of action, it would explain why so many critics have failed to do so.

Jones has been ridiculed for his unsubtleness as a literary critic but, opposed to this, his approach has a naturalness which makes it refreshing.

A. J. A. WALDOCK: *HAMLET: A STUDY IN CRITICAL METHOD* (CAMBRIDGE UNIVERSITY PRESS) 1931

Waldock examines the play by discussing the critics. Valuable both for its short history of *Hamlet* criticism and Waldock's own casual commonsense approach, which is not afraid to disturb the heavy atmosphere of bardolatry with some blustering adverse comments.

JAN KOTT: *SHAKESPEARE OUR CONTEMPORARY* (METHUEN AND CO. LTD). 1964

Hamlet of the Mid-century from this book is offered to the student as a discussion of one modern interpretation of a play which is open to as many interpretations as there are productions. Kott's familiarity with contemporary theatre is his chief recommendation as a critic.

RICHARD L. STERNE: *JOHN GIELGUD DIRECTS RICHARD BURTON IN 'HAMLET'* (HEINEMANN) 1968

Richard Sterne played a minor role in the production and spent his time taping the rehearsals. The resulting book shows the interaction between director and leading actor as a production develops, and gives some insight into how incidental business (props, lighting, costume, grouping etc) can influence the presentation.

Appendix 3

Computer Flow Diagram

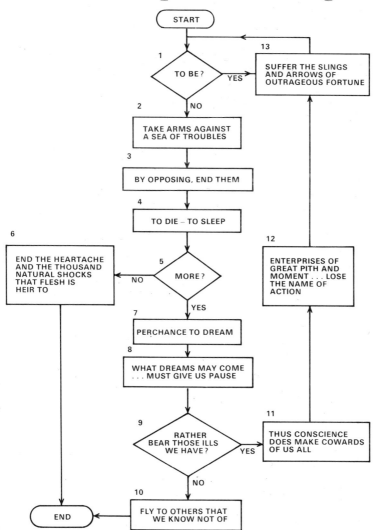